on track ... Horslips

every album, every song

Richard James

sonicbondpublishing.com

on track ...

Horslips

every album, every song

Richard James

sonicbondpublishing.com

Sonicbond Publishing Limited
www.sonicbondpublishing.co.uk
Email: info@sonicbondpublishing.co.uk

First Published in the United Kingdom 2023
First Published in the United States 2023

British Library Cataloguing in Publication Data:
A Catalogue record for this book is available from the British Library

ISBN 978-1-78952-263-1

Typeset in ITC Garamond & ITC Avant Garde
Printed and bound in England

Graphic design and typesetting: Full Moon Media

Author's Note

Unless stated to the contrary, all quotations in this book are from *Horslips – Tall Tales, The Official Biography* by Mark Cunningham, published in 2013 by The O'Brien Press Ltd.

Foreword By Barry Devlin

I've never been formally introduced to Richard James but it turns out he knows me (and the rest of the band) really rather well. That's the power of music, its ability to connect people who've never met, but who share a view of what is pleasing in words and cadences, metaphors and inversions.

A few artists over the years have attracted me to the point that I've listened to everything they've done and tried to figure out why the connection is there. Clive Gregson of Any Trouble; the late Warren Zevon; Lowell George; Colin Harper.

It's nice to think that Richard has brooded as well and has set down his observations. What shines through his work is a thoroughgoing analysis and descriptive clarity. And though his view of the collected works is not uncritical, it's not dispassionate either. There's a genuine liking there for what we did all those years ago.

So let's take this as our formal introduction.

Hello, Richard. Happy to Meet.

Barry Devlin, June 2023

on track ...

Horslips

Contents

Happy to Meet ...

Horslips are the most important band to come out of Ireland. They never attained the broader 'Classic Rock' status of Thin Lizzy, nor became a U2-sized global phenomenon, but it wasn't for lack of trying. The bands significance derives from their invention of a new genre of popular music: 'Celtic Rock'. By taking traditional 'folk' melodies and using them as the basis for new rock songs, sometimes with unusual or unexpected instrumentation and arrangements, they pioneered a style which continues and evolves to this day. During the 1970s, Horslips broke new ground, and introduced audiences across Britain, Europe and America to music which sounded simultaneously both familiar and yet innovative, new and spellbinding.

They were also the first successful rock act to base their entire career in Ireland. They controlled every aspect of their being; stage presentation, graphic design, record pressing, and concert promotion, before it became fashionable. Their blend of progressive rock arrangements with sometimes centuries-old melodies on conceptual albums sought to explain Ireland's past to an audience keen to hear rocked-up versions of ancient narratives that took less than 40 minutes to listen to. Horslips had an impact because, for many Irish people, the band energised them and their sense of identity.

The origins of the band date from 1970 and a Dublin advertising agency called Arks. Devlin, a native of Ardloe, County Tyrone, was a recently arrived copywriter. Eamon Carr, originally from Kells, County Meath, was also a copywriter, and Charles O'Connor, a Middlesborough-born designer all worked there. A forthcoming television advert needed a band to mime along to a pre-recorded song, and the three employees were co-opted into performing for the camera. Realising that another musician was needed, Jim Lockhart, a Dubliner and a friend of Devlin's, was recruited for 'The Gig'. 'The Gentle People', as they were called, duly acted their way through a song promoting Harp lager. Devlin recalled:

> There were free drinks and lots of girls and we thought 'If this is what it's like being in a pop band maybe we should look into this.

As a consequence, the pretend group decided to become a real band. The four men bonded over a shared love of traditional music, and the newly emerging rock scene. They were aware that a guitarist would be needed if they were to develop as a rock band. Kieron 'Spud' Murphy, a photographer at Arks, was swiftly recruited by Devlin to the still-unnamed group, and he is credited with accidentally coming up with the band's name. What started out as a play on 'The Four Horsemen of the Apocalypse' became, after a less than satisfactory rehearsal and a Chinese meal, 'The Four Poxmen of the Horslypse', shortening to 'Horslypse', before finally arriving at Horslips. The band attracted some attention in October when *Spotlight* (Ireland's top music magazine of the time) described them as a 'new rock-orientated group'.

On the DVD *Return of the Danceball Sweethearts,* Carr explained the band's original inspirations:

> A lot of the earlier sort of material we were doing had more in common with what bands were doing in San Francisco in the late Sixties than what was coming out of England, although people would say it's like Steeleye Span, or whatever. I always thought it was much more like The Grateful Dead, or The Joy Of Cooking, or Jefferson Airplane, the bands who mixed up sort of a psychedelic rock thing with Appalachian music, with country blues, with folk and all of that sort of thing.

The band's first official gig, at the CYMS Hall, Navan, County Meath in November, was cancelled when the local curate withdrew his permission, fearing that the evening was 'immoral and designed to seduce the girls of Navan'. Turning disappointment into opportunity, and utilising the skills gained in their day jobs, the band managed to get their name into the press. Fortune smiled on them again when Aine O'Connor (no relation), a friend of Devlin and Carr, offered the band the chance to play on a forthcoming new television series, 'Fonn' for RTE, Ireland's national television station.

By December, Murphy had left to become a photographer with 'Sounds', a London-based weekly rock music magazine. His role was taken by Declan Sinnott, who had played in Carr's previous project, Tara Telephone; a group the drummer described as being 'an Irish version of Pentangle' (the British folk-jazz band). Devlin described the band's vision at this stage:

> We purposely didn't try to emulate what Fairport Convention was doing in the sense that they were English folkies playing rock instruments. We realised that we wanted to do something quite different, which was to deconstruct tunes and use them as the basis for new material.

It is this unique approach to their sources that makes Horslips special.

In January 1971, Gene Mulvaney, also formerly of Tara Telephone, joined the band as bassist. The group became the 'house band' for 'Fonn', performing regularly on its six week run, which aired in February. Devlin recounted:

> We were playing a hybrid of traditional Irish airs and rock'n'roll that was warmly but cautiously received by the audience. No one had ever given Irish music this treatment.

Carr added:

> It was exciting because we had to come up with a couple of new tunes for each performance. It gave us something to work towards, and by the end of the series, we had cracked a repertoire of sorts.

O'Connor mused on the power of the small screen:

> There wasn't much money involved, but the promise of appearing on television was staggering. We had made this abrupt move from the shallow end into the deep end. We didn't want to sing Irish songs but take the melodies that were inherently Irish or Celtic and put them into a different sort of music.

By the time 'Fonn' had finished its run of shows, the band had honed plenty of material, including 'The Clergyman's Lament', 'Johnny's Wedding', 'The Musical Priest', 'Flower Amang Them All', and 'Comb Your Hail And Curl It', into a gig ready set-list. Unlike the vast majority of new bands, the 'Fonn' appearances gave them a national profile, just like that!

By the end of March, Mulvaney had left the group, and bass duties were taken on by Devlin, who moved over from rhythm guitar. The band finally made their first official live debut at Galerie Langlois, Dublin, on 3 April at the same time as the final 'Fonn' programme aired. They played as part of a five-hour 'extravaganza', grandly titled 'Portraits and Anthems'. Such was the response that a second event took place on 1 May. The band then appeared at Sligo Sounds Whit Weekend Festival, where Fairport Convention was headlining. A late addition to the bill was a band called Jeremiah Henry, which featured John Fean on guitar. Horslips and Jeremiah Hardy both appeared at the Clare Festival during the summer.

The Highland Festival in September saw promoter Michael Deeny (who was struck by the band's totally original sound even at this early stage) offering to become their manager. Deeny booked them into Trend Studios in Dublin to record their first track 'Motorway Madness' (which would later resurface on *Tracks From The Vaults*). In October, the band featured on the front cover of *Spotlight* magazine for the first time. By now Horslips were attracting some serious record company attention, including attempts by Decca, Polydor, Transatlantic, and Charisma to sign them. These were resisted; the band were determined to do business on their own terms, and not jump at the first offer so early in their career.

In January 1972, the band recorded 'Johnny's Wedding', 'Flower Amang Them All', and 'Knockeen Free' with Fred Meijer acting as producer. As Deeny was finding it difficult to locate a record company which would be the best fit for his new signing, the band instead formed their own record label, Oats Records. Deeny recollects the freshness and originality of such an approach:

> Oats gave us immense satisfaction and Horslips really knew their stuff. When you pooled their experience in advertising and graphics, their appreciation of rhythm and blues, and pop, and their knowledge of traditional music, what you had was a real force to be reckoned with. It meant we could do everything. So all we had to do was hire a pressing plant for the records, a printer for the sleeves, and a distributor.

In February, the band received their first significant publicity outside of Ireland when a feature on them appeared in the 'Daily Express'. On 17 March (St Patrick's Day), 'Johnny's Wedding' (with 'Flower Amang Them All' as the B-side) was released, and Horslips turned professional. The single spent three weeks on the chart, rising to a highpoint of number ten. Carr recalls:

> The release of 'Johnny's Wedding was the flashpoint. Until then, we'd been this curious, arty collective that had done some TV and a few interesting gigs. But it started to gain momentum. We had started to pick up a following and were regularly hiring an Avis truck to get us to an increasing amount of gigs.

As the band sharpened their musical senses, they also adopted the 'glam rock' look which was popular at the time. This did not impress Sinnott. The final nail in his Horslips career-coffin was another television appearance, where the band again pretended to be a 'pop group' in a commercial for a soft drink manufacturer, Miranda. This was shot at a specially organised concert at Ardmore Studios, Bray, in front of an invited, appropriately 'groovy' audience, where the band mimed to a pre-recorded jingle. Although they were initially against the idea, a significant amount of money was offered for their services, enough to buy a PA system which was suitable for their music and volume required at the venues where they were performing. Temporary pragmatism won out over artistic integrity.

In May, the band played a headlining gig at the National Stadium and whilst it was a success, tensions within the ranks meant that an unhappy Sinnott left on bad terms.

Devlin commented on the guitarist's departure:

> Declan taught me how to be a bass player, so I owe him that much. I know he doesn't have many positive things to say about us and, conversely, I wasn't very enamoured with him as a personality, but I wouldn't deny him his place in the band's history. He must have liked the band enough at the start of it to be in it. We wouldn't have got the band together without Declan, he made a big contribution in that early period, especially as he and Eamon were the two people who had previously been in bands and had an idea of how all that works. He was, and remains, a very good guitar player.

Lockhart was more succinct:

> (Sinnott) wasn't happy being in the band and we weren't happy with him either. It was a relief when he was gone, but filling the vacant position permanently looked like it was going to be a problem.

Gus Guest was drafted in as a replacement. In June, Horslips returned to Trend Studios. 'Green Gravel', 'The Fairy King' and 'Blodau'r Drain' were recorded, and on 25 August, the band's second single 'Green Gravel' (backed with 'The Fairy King') was released.

In July, the band topped the bill at a music festival in Ballyvaughn where, once again, Jeremiah Hardy was performing; Johnny Feans' guitar playing left an indelible impression on the Horslips collective eye and ear. In August, their second single was released, reaching the top 20 in its first week, and in the autumn, Guest left, but on good terms. Fean was invited to audition for the band, having been head-hunted by O'Connor, who travelled by taxi from Dublin to Shannon to find the guitarist. On 1 October, Fean officially joined the band, playing his first gig with them at the National Stadium later that month. In November, work began on what would become the band's debut album.

The mixture of Northern and Southern Irish members, together with an import from the northeast of England, meant that Horslips was a band without borders. Their existence challenged the North/South 'them and us' attitude; they were playing Irish-flavoured rock music for anybody and everybody who wanted to hear it. Lockhart confirmed this viewpoint in an interview with Ralph McLean on BBC Radio Ulster in March 2022, saying:

> Charles had come over from Middlesborough, where he had been playing in the College of Art Ceilidh band. I was playing tin whistles and playing trad stuff. Barry had come down from around Loch Neagh with all these songs from around the loch, Eamon's grandfather had been in a ceilidh band, I think, or had a ceilidh band, and then later when Johnny came on board, he had been playing banjo around Clare with Ted Furey and mandolin and so there was in parallel with all the rock'n'roll influences there was always these traditional influences coming in that we'd all been intimately involved in.

In broad terms, O'Connor and Fean were the traditional folk players. Lockhart had training in jazz and classical piano arrangements. Devlin and Carr had strong leanings towards the rockier side of things, and all of them loved The Beatles. Lockhart saw that the fusion of traditional Irish melodies within a modern-day rock setting as a major factor in the band's success:

> We had different angles of approach for blending in Irish influences. In some cases, we would take an Irish tune and use it as the main riff so that it made it do something unexpected. The riff would generate a chord structure and then you'd superimpose a song on top of it, making sure that the two elements sat comfortably together. Another approach was to take a tune and use it as a countermelody, as we did in 'Ghosts', and 'Sideways to the Sun'. The tune is set up, and once a chordal framework is set, the tune acts as a counterpoint to the vocal melody, with both starting at different times and forming a complimentary relationship where disparate elements illuminate each other. That was always a very satisfying way of writing.

Happy to Meet, Sorry to Part (1972)

Personnel:
Eamon Carr: drums, bodhran, percussion
Barry Devlin: bass, vocals
Johnny Fean: electric and acoustic guitars
Charles O'Connor: fiddle, mandolin, concertina, vocals
Jim Lockhart: keyboards, generation whistle, concert flute, vocals
All tracks composed and/or arranged by Carr, Devlin, Fean, O'Connor, and Lockhart
Recorded on the Rolling Stones Mobile at Longfield House, County Tipperary, Ireland
Produced and engineered by Alan O'Duffy and Horslips
Mixed at Olympic Studios, London, November 1972
Released on: 4 December 1972
Issued on Oats Records in Ireland (M003), RCA Records in the UK (M003), and Atco SD in USA (7030)

In 1972, no studio in Ireland had the capacity to record 24 separate tracks of sound. Whilst the band could have headed to England to record, Deeny and Carr suggested that they hire the Rolling Stones Mobile, which was duly placed on a ferry and delivered to Longfield House, an eighteenth-century building in County Tipperary. Speaking on the *Dancehall Sweethearts,* DVD Devlin said:

> We were aware of the potential value of being the first people to bring in a 24-track to Ireland. No 24-track existed in Ireland so we trundled it across the Irish Sea. It was actually a great stroke, I mean, the *Evening Herald* did a series of double-page spreads, everyone came down and we entertained them, and everyone had a great time and they came back and wrote about this extraordinary, funny, and interesting thing that was happening down in Longfield House, County Tip.

Ian Stewart, the manager of the mobile studio, recommended Alan O'Duffy as a producer to Deeny. O'Duffy already had an impressive CV, including two albums for The Rolling Stones, *Let It Bleed* (1969) and *Sticky Fingers* (1971).

Rehearsals took place at the Deeny family holiday home in County Donegal. The sessions attracted the attention of both the Irish press (particularly Dublin's *Evening Herald*) and the weekly English music newspaper *Melody Maker*. The album was recorded on a very tight budget, with money being saved as O'Duffy wore the simultaneous hats of engineer and producer. Different rooms of the spacious house were used, including the cellars and the library, and bales of hay were brought in to separate the sounds of the individual instruments.

With recording completed, the tapes were quickly mixed at Olympic Studios in Barnes, London, and the finished album was released in Ireland in time for Christmas. It would be the fastest-selling LP in the country until the commercial juggernaut, which was ABBA reached their peak towards the end of the decade.

The album cover was ambitious, expensive, and difficult to produce. Based upon an eight-sided concertina with the band members visible through the instrument's keyholes, it was also a gatefold design, with additional pages inserted within. The cost of this presentation was probably more than the budget for the recording, but it was a visual statement of originality to match the musical content, and a testament to the band's vision.

The album sleeve is an elaborate, impressive affair. The front featured the band posing in front of a damaged Celtic cross in the Irish countryside against a backdrop of a foreboding sky. As if to emphasise the fusion of the old and the new, the band (left to right, it's O'Connor, Fean, Carr, Devlin, and Lockhart) are all standing, wearing the fashionable clothing of the time – it's all flares, long hair, and sparkly, garishly coloured 'glam-rock' apparel. Inside, the band is pictured individually; Lockhart looks mean and moody, sitting in-between two pianos. Overleaf Fean is pictured lost in thought and sheepskin in a soft focus shot. On the next page, Devlin, sporting a magnificent droopy moustache, is doing his best impression of a bouncer, with arms folded. Carr is seated, reading a book, and drinking a (possibly unfortunate) cup of tea. O'Connor has a pixie-like demeanour as he sits against a wall, surrounded by the instruments he plays on the album. The lyrics to the songs are also included, and the rear page of the sleeve has another view of the cross with the band in the distance, grouped together, looking towards it. At least the weather has improved.

The band logo, always an integral part of a long-term identity, is a curious amalgam of pseudo-Celtic lettering meets Roger Dean's 'flow and join' style used on most of Yes's album covers of the 1970s. It is again the marriage of traditional and modern looks which adds to the mystique of what this album might actually sound like, as old and new visuals collide.

When *Happy to Meet ...* was released, demand was overwhelming. The first pressing of 35,000 copies sold out very quickly, partly because the fusion of traditional and rock genres was so fresh and compelling, but also because Horslips were the real deal; an Irish band, playing a new type of Irish music, recording and gigging in Ireland. Of course, success breeds criticism. Lockhart remembered:

> The album was a fantastic lift-off. However, a lot of the folk purists that had now started to become aware of us were righteously apoplectic. They were fiercely protective of the tradition and viewed what we were doing to 'their' music as vandalism like we were drawing a moustache on the 'Mona Lisa'. But equally, we saw that we were bringing the music to an audience who were never likely to hear it, let alone embrace it.

O'Connor supports this:

> There was never any disrespect from our side towards the 'trad' brigade. We were like punk folkers without really knowing it, and I think that really appealed to young people who loved seeing all these old-timers getting wound up.

The band's youth and relative inexperience meant that the music on Happy to Meet is daring and ground-breaking. Being largely new to the concept of being a rock band they believed anything was, and should be, possible. If, as Lockhart puts it, knowledge can be 'the great inhibitor of creativity', Horslips' collective innocence was a consequent and substantial strength. The band received favourable press coverage for their innovative approach and style. A headline typical of the time, in the *Evening Herald* ran:

> Horslips: the band whose blend of space rock and traditional Irish music could make them the new name to watch.

Devlin, talking on the *Danceball Sweetbearts* DVD, said:

> *Happy to Meet, Sorry to Part* is an odd album in the sense that when we were doing it we already knew that we were going to do *The Táin*. Jethro Tull's first album was called *This Was* (1968) because in a way it encompassed the stuff that they'd been doing for the two years up to that, and the same is true of *Happy to Meet, Sorry to Part*. It encapsulated what we'd been doing from October 1970.

'Happy to Meet' (0.48)
Anyone who's ever been to a traditional music session will recognise that the mood and instrumentation of this short opening jig which was taken from 'O'Neill's *The Music of Ireland*. Almost certainly the only opening album track ever to be recorded in a library, ('quiet, please!'), some concertina noodling, interspersed with a bout of coughing, quickly leads into a brisk melody on concertina, joined by banjo, tin whistle and bodhran, which fades quickly away. It sets a scene, but 'Happy to Meet' is deceptive; this is not going to be anyone's usual idea of what a traditional music album would sound like...

'Hall of Mirrors' (5.29)
A swirling fairground organ sound plays a suitably cheery melody with touches of psychedelia in 6/8 time which turns into a disturbing diminished arpeggio, replete with distant percussion. This gradually fades to leave a single sustained keyboard note under which the song itself starts proper with an arpeggiated riff. Over this, the guitar and electric mandolin add decorative

touches with some subtle, spacious bass before the first verse of Carr's lyrics: 'Once you've been through the Tunnel Of Love it's the Hall of Mirrors for you'. The restrained atmosphere is destroyed by the explosive chorus ('As soon as you're through the welcome door, it's much more fun on your own...') with effective backing vocals and tight drum work.

The second verse sees a return to relative calm, with increased bass and drum contributions. This time, the chorus section is sung without a substantial increase in volume, and this is followed by an instrumental section where guitar feedback sustain blends effectively with electric mandolin to produce an unsettling mood. Surprisingly, the opening keyboard melody returns briefly at 3.15, and the third verse and chorus feature a disappointing repeat of the opening lyrics.

At 4.08, the pace quickens with a rapid-fire semiquaver five-note guitar flurry which climbs in pitch as it is played four times, accompanied by vicious staccato drumming, leading into the final words: 'Hall of Mirrors, it's fun inside, Hall of Mirrors, takes you down to size, Hall of Mirrors where you can't hide from yourself'. The song accelerates into a second instrumental where Fean impresses with his tuneful, overdriven solo (4.25 – 5.09). A reprise of the fast semiquaver sequence leads into a repeat of the final section of lyrics, which builds through a crescendo into a tight ending.

As a statement of intent, 'Hall Of Mirrors' lays out Horslips' early style with conviction and imagination. Yes, the sound is very much 'of its time,' but there is plenty of creativity and style in this track to keep ears interested as the album develops…

'The Clergyman's Lamentation' (4.39)

This instrumental starts slowly and calmly with the electric mandolin playing graceful arpeggios, while melodic bass and an expressive, clean electric guitar tone fill the soundscape. In the background, the spooky 'fairground sound' from 'Hall of Mirrors' swoops and swirls quietly.

After 40 seconds, this is all swept away, replaced by the central melody played slowly on electric mandolin, with acoustic guitar providing chord accompaniment. Bass joins as the tune progresses. At 1.23, the melody gathers pace before being joined by tin whistle and bodhran.

At 2.19, the ghostly organ from 'Hall of Mirrors' returns as the pace slows and a new melody harmonised between mandolin, electric guitar and keyboards takes over at 2.39. Triplet-based drums add to the sense of tension and anticipation, and some wah-wah guitar chords (cleverly mixed back and forth into opposing stereo channels) lead to a reprise of the initial tune on mandolin. Carr powers along behind the bass and electric guitar, whilst the organ provides a constant texture in the background. A repeat of the 'wah-wah' sequence leads into the coda section which is a mixture of organ, bass meanderings and fading drumming. This gradually fades away, leaving just the organ playing to the close.

Comparing the Horslips arrangement to the original slow air, written by Turlough O'Carolan (1670 – 1738), shows just how far the band were prepared to take Irish music in a new, exciting and, to some, challenging direction. Whilst the central melodies are retained, everything else (tempo, texture, instrumentation, dynamics) undergoes a massive transformation. This 'Clergyman's Lamentation', like so much of the material on the album, is an impressive display of instrumental virtuosity, creative arrangement, and inspired musicianship.

'An Bratach Ban' (2.04)

'An Bratach Ban' is a Scottish tune introduced to the band by Lockhart, who also sings the Gaelic lyrics. The track incorporates two other melodies: 'Rolling In The Long Grass' and 'Kitty Got A Clinker Coming From The Races'.

The original's restrained tempo, and occasionally twee interpretation, is given the full Horslips treatment, opening with an unexpected reggae rhythm led by syncopated bass, plus some very quiet organ and guitar. The main melody is played on violin and mandolin before the vocals appear. The second section of words has the accompaniment dropping down to just percussion and mandolin which provides an interesting contrast.

After only 48 seconds, the tune moves up several gears and into double time for very brief diversions into 'Rolling in the Long Grass' (0.48 – 1.02), and 'Kitty Got a Clinker Coming From the Races' (1.03 – 1.17) with prominent and entertaining contributions on acoustic guitar, fiddle, and finally banjo. The arrangement and feel of these inclusions are those of a riotous ceilidh. The vocals and original feel then return for the balance of the song, with the second lyric section again featuring the 'drop out' instrumentation as this rousing number goes into a long fade.

'The Shamrock Shore' (4.34)

This evergreen song is given a subtle, gentle reinterpretation with a sustained keyboard tone, concertina and acoustic guitar dominating the first four phrases of the introduction. Fean adds some tasteful slide guitar fills, and bass is added to the texture for the second set of phrases.

Devlin sings with restraint, his vocal melody being hauntingly matched by the uilleann pipes. Harmony vocals join for the second half of the verse with the ensuing instrumental (2.42 – 3.34) featuring subtle melodic slide guitar fills. At times, Fean matches the underlying pipe melody then his playing becomes more bluesy. The effect is evocative, beguiling and hypnotic. It's like listening to a Celtic version of 'Albatross' (Fleetwood Mac), a tranquil, beautiful sound that transports the listener effortlessly to another place.

Halfway through the second verse, the instruments all drop out, leaving just the pipes and highly effective harmonised vocals, the top line of which is sung by producer O'Duffy. The instruments rejoin for the final lyrics, which slow, bringing this island of musical peace to a close.

'Flower Amang Them All' (2.04)

The pastoral mood continues. 'Flower Amang Them All', originally written by Sir John Fenwick (1645-1697), is a traditional song from the north of England, and was introduced to the band by O'Connor. Originally recorded as the B side of 'Johnny's Wedding' (which would appear later on *Tracks From The Vaults*), the track was re-recorded for inclusion on the album.

It begins with a melancholy concertina melody which is joined by tin whistle. The texture grows with bass, acoustic guitar, and percussion. The counterpoint and harmonies between the lead instruments are extremely effective, and the tune meanders along pleasantly in a soothing manner. The piece ends on an imperfect cadence, creating an appropriate level of anticipation, given what is about to hit the ears ...

'Bim Istigh Ag Ol' (3.38)

In its original instrumental version, this tune is known as 'Comb Your Hair and Curl It'; the Gaelic title translating as 'I'm Always Inside Drinking'.

The introduction is atmospheric; harmonised whistles, bass, cymbal swells, gently picked electric mandolin and a tambourine all contribute until, after 36 seconds, the mood changes abruptly with a fast melody on the mandolin, which leads into the rousing vocals sung by Lockhart in Gaelic.

At 1.20, an instrumental section takes over; it's stirring stuff with a suitably manic rock feel throughout. A bluesy guitar solo and manic triplet-based drumming are the stand-out features of this tightly arranged track, where each instrument has a significant part to play. At 2.09, the music changes again with an electric mandolin solo put through a wah-wah pedal, whilst syncopated power chords smashes provide a heavy backdrop.

The vocals return at 2.39 with some impressive harmonies. Tin whistle, fiddle, banjo, and guitar join in the melody, and the sonic mayhem really kicks in as the track blasts into an accelerating coda, reaching a 'typical-of-its-time' heavy rock ending. It's all tremendous fun, played with passion and precision in equal measure.

'Furniture' (5.14)

This is the album's big rock ballad, one which in a live setting would leave plenty of room for instrumental exploration. The words were written by Lockhart, who said:

> The lyrics of 'Furniture' started out as a poem that I'd written about my parents, and how tolerant they were about me abandoning my academic career in favour of playing in a band. It's a very metaphorical song in the vein of 'Whiter Shade Of Pale' in the sense that you really need to know the background to understand what the hell it's about.

The introduction is another excellent blend of flute (playing the melody) with support from acoustic guitar, bass and drums. The lyrics are impressive, if occasionally opaque: 'Solid as a chair from an older time, you watched me slowly grow away from you, only half understood the things I had to do, but you let me try although it brought the pain to you' and, for the second verse, 'Badly beaten by the troubles you'd had to bear, you invested everything you had in me, hoping I would hoist your flag for all to see. But I broke the things you cherished so carefully'. Devlin sings throughout with great sensitivity and phrasing.

The song builds with a sustained organ into the chorus: 'The best and oldest furniture cannot be rearranged. If it suits the way it is, there is no need to change. The best and straightest arrow is the one that will range, out of the archer's view'. Fean's tastefully bluesy fills at the front of the mix add to the mood.

Following the second verse and chorus, the song moves into an instrumental section featuring a new riff-based melody. This is a new interpretation of the traditional tune 'Oro Se Do Bheatha Bhaile'. It is played in unison four times over, in which Fean introduces a distorted solo with the organ adding moody arpeggios. The riff then mutates, which gradually calms into a repeat of the chorus. The effect of this is heightened by the inclusion of harmony vocals, swirling keyboards, and piano arpeggios.

At 4.14, we're into a reprise of the instrumental section, where the underlying riff is played simultaneously on uilleann pipes and electric guitar repeatedly until the song comes to a heroic and heavy conclusion.

'Ace and Deuce' (3.32)

There's a complete change of mood here with this brisk acoustic guitar and harpsichord-based tune, also known as 'The Ace and Deuce of Pipering'. Joined by bass and percussion for the second run-through of the melody, 48 seconds in, the music takes a more reflective turn with some finger-style acoustic guitar playing. Bass, electric guitar, and percussion slide in and out again for a repeat of the section, before the music becomes more brooding and dramatic.

The key shifts from G major to a progression of E major, D major, C major seventh and D major chords, with the melody transferring to the violin as organ, bass, vigorously strummed guitar, and bodhran all add to the atmosphere. The mood brightens at 1.54 with a return to the introductory theme, with bass and percussion as prominent in the mix as the guitar and keyboard.

At 2.20, a new violin-led melody takes centre stage together with some clever counterpoint lines on the electric guitar, bass, and harmony from the keyboards. The tone is celebratory, putting the listener in mind of a wedding, possibly, until the brooding, darker feel returns at 3.02, building and building this intricate instrumental to a dramatic close.

'Dance to Your Daddy' (4.37)

O'Connor's North-East England roots are given full rein on this track, although you would never guess it until the vocals begin as the instrumentation is anything but traditional.

A staccato keyboard refrain is joined by more keyboards playing a counter melody at differing octaves with bass joining, as the song takes familiar form with a violin melody. Sung by O'Connor, the vocals ('You shall have a fishy on a little dishy...') sound like the band are trying their best to keep the smile off their faces as they record. While the music may be light-hearted and upbeat in delivery, the arrangement is again razor sharp, with well-placed backing harmonies and precise playing from the rhythm section.

This is nowhere better exemplified than in the instrumental section (1.54 – 3.03) where Fean employs blues, country and even jazz stylings into his lightly overdriven tone against a syncopated and busy backing. At 3.04, the vocals return, with the backing vocals becoming more noticeable. Lockhart throws in brief flute and tin whistle flourishes alongside O'Connor's violin, as the track sails towards a delightful end, full of melody, brio, and humour. The degree of musical skill and dexterity involved in taking a straightforward folk song and transforming it into a multi-layered arrangement is not to be underestimated.

'Scallaway Rip-Off' (1.52)

The opening held chord soon powers into this jaunty instrumental, which is so titled as it incorporates both 'The Scallaway Lasses' and 'The De'els Take the Minister'. Sounding like it belongs in a pub during a busy late-night session, the background noises (shouting, whooping, clapping) were provided by everyone else who was staying at Longfield House during the recording sessions.

Lockhart's tin whistle is the lead instrument, playing in unison with the fiddle. This is Horslips at their most 'traditional', with only the electric guitar and bass hinting at what is to come. Thirty-nine seconds in, energetic drumming soon lifts the music onto a higher level, where it stays for the track's duration, coming to a predictable conclusion. 'Scallaway Rip-Off' is magnificent; good humoured, and, of course, superbly played.

'The Musical Priest' (4.31)

A meandering introduction of wah-wah'd electric guitar, mandolin arpeggios and a distant bass is soon being pummelled by relentless drums, which drive the music into a steady 4/4 rhythm, with the organ providing the melody, which again had been sourced from 'O' Neills'.

There is a busy electric mandolin solo (1.07–1.52), with Fean adding occasional harmony moments, until the music accelerates rapidly into a much more energetic section. Here, the organ plays a furious new tune with dramatic rhythmic stabs from bass and drums, until a bluesy, phaser-effect heavy guitar solo (2.38 – 3.20). This mixes tasteful phrases with intensity, building the mood into an explosion of melody for mandolin and keyboard.

At this point, the pace becomes positively frenetic with some exemplary playing, fast, powerful, and controlled. The energy and accuracy are as impressive as the breathtaking tempo, the tune coming to a brisk, tight end. Fifty years on, this section of 'The Musical Priest' remains stunning. What it must have been like to hear this album for the first time in early 1970s Ireland explains the band's instant and well-deserved popularity.

'Sorry to Part' (1.27)

This longer version of the opening track dispenses with the 'pub' atmosphere of its companion. 'Sorry To Part' is taken at a slightly slower tempo and begins cohesively rather than the ad-hoc feel of its first appearance. The music motors along to a gradual fade, powered along by the bodhran.

In *On The Record* (Mark Cunningham, 2022), Devlin said;

> 'In a general sense, like a lot of debut albums, ours was a snapshot of where we had been over the previous two years, but we were already pressing on at a hell of a pace, so to us, the material was already old before it came out. We were itching to take a big leap forward.'

And leap they did ...

The Táin (1973)

Personnel:
Eamon Carr: drums, bodhran, percussion
Barry Devlin: bass, vocals
John Fean: guitar, banjo, vocals
Jim Lockhart: keyboards, flute, whistles, Uileann pipes, vocals
Charles O'Connor: fiddle, mandolin, concertina, vocals
Recorded at The Manor, and Escape Studios
Mixed at Olympic Studios, September 1973
Produced by Alan O'Duffy and Horslips
Engineered by Alan O'Duffy
All tracks composed/arranged by Carr, Devlin, Fean, O'Connor, and Lockhart
Released on 23 November 1973
Issued on Oats Records in Ireland (M005), RCA Records in the UK (M005) 18 January 1974, and Atco SD in USA (7039)

On 19 April, Horslips played their first concert in England at the Conway Hall, Holborn, London. The gig became the catalyst for the band landing a lucrative international distribution deal with Atlantic Records. Late April saw recording sessions for the follow-up to *Happy to Meet* commence at The Manor Studios in Oxfordshire. On 30 April, the band released a new single: 'Dearg Doom' with 'The High Reel' on the B-side. It got to number eight in the Irish singles charts as part of a seven-week run. 'The High Reel' had been recorded during the sessions for *Happy to Meet* but hadn't made the final selection, although subsequent pressings would include this 'new' track. The high-energy instrumental would finally surface in its own right on *Tracks From the Vaults*. Excerpts from *The Táin* were first played live at a concert at the National Stadium, Dublin.

Horslips undertook a short British tour in July and released their first UK single, 'The High Reel' paired with 'Furniture', via RCA on 20 July. Mid-August found the band at Escape Studios in Kent working further on *The Táin*. In October, they recorded a session for Radio One's *Top Gear* programme featuring 'An Bratach Ban', 'Dearg Doom', and 'Maeve's Court'. The band then toured the United Kingdom in the autumn, supporting Steeleye Span, and that other well-respected pioneer of 'Folk-Rock', Suzi Quatro. Two UK singles promoted the forthcoming album: 'Dearg Doom' (with 'The Shamrock Shore' on the B-side), and 'More Than You Can Chew' paired with 'Faster Than the Hound' were UK releases on 19 October 1973, and 29 March 1974 respectively.

For a band to release a fully-fledged concept album, especially one based on an ancient Irish legend, at this early stage of their career, was another sign of their ambition and vision. Whilst the 1970s was the decade where such ventures were fashionable, it was Horslips' choice of subject matter which marked them out as being strikingly original. With *The Táin*, Horslips presented a musical documentary of the Cattle Raid of Cooley, a famous legend of Irish literature whose story revolves around a conflict between the provinces of Ulster and Connaught in pre-Christian Ireland over a prize bull. It is the centrepiece of the 'Ulster Cycle of Heroic Tales', with the events believed to be set in approximately 500 BC. The earliest version of the story is contained in *The Book of the Dun Cow,* which dates from the twelfth century; prior to that, the legend was kept alive by storytellers over the generations. In terms of academic and historical importance, *The Táin* ranks with the epic poem by Virgil, 'The Aeneid'.

The band had first looked at *The Táin* as a possible subject for an album in 1971. With the dust settling after *Happy to Meet...*, the band revisited some of their ideas, composed largely by Devlin and Lockhart, for a theatre project on the same subject, and then decided to focus on the story as a single whole album project. O'Connor remembers:

> When we were planning our first album, we thought about doing a conceptual piece, although it didn't happen until *The Táin*. Barry and Jimmy were into pop/rock, Johnny and I were interested in the traditional elements, as was Jimmy, and Eamon was the poet. We found that organising a conceptual album was a way of pulling five people together and harnessing strengths. We were delighted that the album's eclectic flavour captured our true essence.

Carr explained his version of the tale and the album lyrics:

> There are several versions of *The Táin*, the most famous being Thomas Kinsella's contemporary interpretation with Louis Le Brocquy's beautiful wash drawings. Purposefully I didn't refer to Kinsella's translation because it was too current. I preferred to go back to different source materials and take out my own highlights of the story to try and set up pivotal action points. Initially, I dragged in various versions and retellings of the yarn. Among the devices I employed were attempts at weaving in strands of a Cu Chulainn narrative as described in the plays of W. B. Yeats, whose son, Michael, was very generous in ensuring that we had permission to use the marvellous quote by W. B. on the back of the original album sleeve. It helped explain why I thought the story might have a contemporary resonance. This was a time when concept albums were hip and happening, so it didn't seem like a bad idea.

The Yeats quote, taken from 'Preface to Lady Gregory's Cuchulainn of Muirthemne' published in March 1902, to which Carr refers, reads:

> We Irish should keep these personages much in our hearts, for they lived in the places where we ride and go marketing, and sometimes they have met one another on the hills that cast their shadows upon our doors at evening.

The story of the album *The Táin* is as follows: one night in bed, the promiscuous Connacht Queen Maeve quarrels with her husband, Ailill, over who is the wealthiest. Not liking the suggestion that he is a kept man, Ailill's magnificent white bull is the deciding factor in their subsequent comparisons of value.

Maeve doesn't like to lose and so dispatches her messenger, MacRoth, to Cooley to rent the famed brown bull for a year, thus giving her the advantage. The Bull's owner agrees to the idea until MacRoth and his party gets very drunk, and reveal that if the owner had refused, they would have taken the animal by force anyway. The deal is dead and MacRoth returns empty-handed.

Maeve decides to go to war. She marshalls all her warriors and allies from Munster and Tara, including Ailill's six brothers and their armies. She receives favourable omens from the Druids and the long march to Cooley begins. A sorceress appears and warns Maeve of impending defeat at the hands of 'Dearg Doom', Cu Chulainn. She ignores the warning.

Meanwhile, the men of Ulster are ill with labour pains, the legacy of a curse placed upon them for their treatment of a pregnant woman. The only man not affected is Cu Chulainn, whose very birth is shrouded in secrecy. Single-handedly, he takes on the defence of Ulster, harassing Maeve's soldiers. As the Connaught losses grow greater, the deposed King of Ulster, Fergus MacRoich (who is Maeve's secret lover) meets Cu Chulainn and arranges a treaty.

Cu Chulainn agrees to single-handed combat with any Connaught champion, provided Maeve's army does not advance. One by one, day after day, he defeats each warrior until eventually, he faces his old foster brother, and close friend, Ferdia. Cu Chulainn pleads with Ferdia to leave, but he refuses and they continue to fight each other for three days. Finally, Cu Chulainn flies into a rage and slays his friend with a supernatural javelin, Gae Bolga. As Ferdia falls, Cu Chulainn catches him and carries him to the riverbank. Overcome with despair, Cu Chulainn abandons the fight and Maeve's army moves south with the stolen bull.

The Ulster men rally and, joined again by Cu Chulainn, give chase. The Morrigan, Queen of Demons, who has been encouraging slaughter all along, predicts the outcome. In the battle which follows, the Connaught army is routed. Maeve's life is spared by Cu Chulainn. As the Ulster men are taking the brown bull home, they encounter Ailill's white bull. The two bulls fight with the brown bull finally victorious. The armies consider destroying him, the cause of all their suffering, but leave him dying as he staggers homewards.

Of course, it is not necessary to know the story of *The Táin* to enjoy the album's many strengths. Carr's clever and inventive lyrics give the tale a modern accessibility, and the band hone 'their sound' in style. Whilst two of the six album's instrumentals are purely scene-setting devices, akin to film scores, they work very well in their own right. The other four are fine examples of highly skilled musicianship and arrangement to produce tightly integrated pieces of music which show the band at an early peak of their career. And, of course, *The Táin* contains, alongside many excellent songs, 'Dearg Doom'; a track that is quintessential Horslips, and, for many fans, their best.

The album cover, another O'Connor design, is a striking image; a raised silver right fist with a ring on the index finger, the wrist wrapped in chain mail is set against a black background. The artist explained the visuals:

> *The Táin* wasn't as complex as *Happy to Meet*, but it had its own manufacturing difficulties. It's probably our most iconic design because the fist is such a strong Celtic image, with male aggression suggested by the chain mail. That was actually a British-style demi-glove and not medieval or Celtic. But as soon as I spotted it, I saw its potential as cover art. That's my fist. We didn't realise that by spraying my hand silver and dressing it with the chain mail, it would look as silver as it does on the printed sleeve. The texture against the black background was just perfect.

The band logo, hand drawn by Billy Moore, was one of many different styles used for their name for their 1970s output. It would be, however, this *Táin* logo which would become the defining image following the reformation in the 21st century.

Perhaps it's the striking monochrome cover, maybe it's the degree of reverberation and echo added to many of the tracks by O'Duffy, but *The Táin* comes across as a very 'dark' sounding album. Many of the songs are set in minor keys, but there are also moments of lightness and levity which provide essential balance to this highly impressive work.

The Táin is an album of massive ambition, with an almost complete disregard for what should or should not be done with rock music, and for some fans the group's finest work. Bold, adventurous, sometimes plain weird, and frequently outstanding, it set a benchmark for the band's talents. Of course, it would have been tempting for them to follow it with *The Táin 2*; but every Horslips album showed a divergence, a progression (for good or ill), and a willingness to break new musical ground. Certainly, in the first arc of the Horslips history (1972 – 1975) this is the band at their most wide-ranging, confident, and spellbinding. In the *BBC Radio Ulster* interview with Ralph McLean, Devlin attested to this:

> *The Táin* for me is the most exciting in many ways because we were completely overreaching ourselves. We were trying to do things that we weren't technically qualified to do and we had notions above ourselves. With *The Táin* we thought 'we can do anything' and it was wonderful.

'Setanta' (1.52)

The first of two scene-setting instrumentals, 'Setanta', is a tense and disturbing piece which takes its title from Cu Chulainn's birth name. As an atmospheric prelude, it does its job well; the sound effects transporting us back to a mythical past, a curtain being opened by modern instrumentation to reveal an age-old story.

A discordant series of descending notes on a swirling organ is quickly subsumed by some distorted climbing triplet phrases (with a heavy degree of reverberation) around which vigorous snare drumming moves constantly between the left and right stereo channels.

At 1.03, a doom-laden heavy guitar riff and rhythm section kicks in with the theme, which will continue to appear until Cu Chulainn kills Ferdia. This section has similarities to the early music of Black Sabbath in its dark, descending progression. Again, the level of reverb added increases the uneasy atmosphere. At 1.37, the rising guitar triplets and drums return and fade as a solitary concertina melody segues into ...

'Maeve's Court' (1.40)

... and we are back into *Happy to Meet* territory with O'Connor playing the traditional Irish tune 'Knockeen Free' on the concertina. The tune was taken from Joyce's 1873 collection *Ancient Irish Music*. The track places the listener at the hill fort in Connaught, the seat of Queen Maeve, who is about to set the action in motion. Joined by flutes (0.16), acoustic guitar (0.32), bass (0.50), and finally, bodhran (1.07),

This is a highly melodic, tightly arranged piece with excellent counterpoint phrases and harmonies between the instruments. The pastoral mood is in direct contrast with the *sturm unt drang* of 'Setanta', and again the music blends into the next track by switching time signature from a brisk 4/4 into a lilting 6/8 section as it becomes...

'Charolais' (4.03)

'Charlolais' begins with just the concertina playing a repeated two-bar melody. This is soon joined by sustained keyboards, a flute with an alternate melody, and a slightly distorted electric guitar playing a variation of the flute tune. All three melodic lines co-exist and where the higher-pitched, syncopated bass line begins, the music moves into 2/4 time, and a rockier sound takes hold with the addition of drums.

Devlin's vocals recount the marital quarrel, which opens the story: 'Her words were sharp, they cut him deep, in a war between the sheets. But when he brought his bull to her, it meant a woman making war – beyond the eiderdown!' The humouress slant to the words mirrors the eccentric narrative style of the source material. Carr takes a lyrical liberty by substituting the Brown Bull for the modern and gentle-natured Charolais, which did not exist in pre-Christian Ireland. There is a robust, distorted guitar counter-melody alongside the vocals.

The central melody of the song is the traditional 'Rosc Catha na Mumhan' ('The Battle Hymn of Munster'), and the chorus is a cracker ('Charolais,

Charolais, we are come for you today. The champions and the seven sons are come to take away the Donn'). Throughout the song, traditional and modern elements blend effortlessly, with the flute and electric guitar getting equal billing in the mix. The keyboard interjections in the chorus are particularly impressive.

Following the second chorus, there is an excellent, flamboyant flute solo (2.15 – 3.11) which then leads into a biting lead guitar section (2.48 – 3.11), the music growing progressively heavier and louder as it reaches a climax. After another chorus, the third verse lays plain the sorcerer's prophecy: 'But the Fairy Child knew more, saw the host stained red in war, saw the hero, light around the head of a dragon boy just ripe for bed of wives and manly sons'. The final chorus is sung *a cappella;* the instrumentation vanishes, leaving some very impressive three-part harmonisation.

'Charolais' is an absolute belter of a tune, and encapsulates the Horslips approach; storytelling with a highly melodic spine mixes effortlessly with clever, intricate arrangement, skilled playing, and a unique fusion of the old and the new.

'The March' (1.34)

The album's third instrumental opens with some tight, militaristic snare drumming. Lockhart plays the main melody, which is a further interpretation of 'Rosc Catha na Mumhan', on the tin whistle, with bass and guitar joining for the repeated refrain. When the main melody is reprised, Fean adds some tasteful parallel fifth harmonies before the track breaks into a new melody on the electric mandolin.

At 1.07, the mood changes and the tempo slows slightly as harmonised flutes play a further new melody. Joined by bass, guitar and drums, with uplifting stabs from the organ, the counter melody becomes dominant. The music grows in intensity, suddenly cutting straight into ...

'You Can't Fool The Beast' (3.45)

Quoted from the album's sleeve notes:

> There has always been great speculation as to the nature of the Brown Bull. In the manuscripts, the Bull is referred to as 'an Donn Cuailgne'. While the word 'Donn' means 'brown', it is also the name of the ancient Irish God of the dead. There is also a related story which tells how two malevolent magicians take the shape of Bulls and resume a long-standing feud.

'You Can't Fool the Beast' is a pacy, busy acoustic guitar-led song, with the flute throwing in plenty of fills in-between Devlin's vocals. The chorus is another catchy melodic section which consists of two bars of 4/4 time followed by a bar of 3/4 time, which is repeated, with impressive backing harmonies adding to the texture. A second verse and chorus lead into an instrumental section with a classy bluesy guitar solo (1.54 – 2.20) which is set over the verse's chord structure.

O'Connor takes over on violin using a variation of the chorus chord progression as the basis for his contribution (2.21 – 2.48). After the third verse, the final chorus is left hanging in the air on a D major chord (the song is in the key of E minor), leaving a sense of anticipation of what is to come ...

'Dearg Doom' (3.05)

...which, of course, is utterly magnificent. An instant classic, a song destined for an appearance on any and every compilation of the band's work, and a concert favourite guaranteed to get the audience going.

'Dearg Doom' is the finest three minutes (and five seconds) of the band's first half of the 1970s. Using the sixteenth-century traditional tune 'O'Neill's Cavalry' as the basis of the all-conquering guitar riff, 'Dearg Doom' is, not only Cu Chulainn's anthem, but, in more recent times, it was used as part of 'Put 'Em Under Pressure', the song of the Republic of Ireland's FIFA world cup campaign in 1990.

Interviewed on the *The Road to the O2* DVD, Carr remembers the difficult gestation of this now classic song:

> When we started, we weren't natural musicians, well, not Barry and I, we weren't a natural rhythm section, but we were willing to experiment. In terms of 'Dearg Doom', Johnny came up with this astonishing riff and the day I heard him playing it I said to him 'That's an incredible riff, we have to have that'. So we knocked up a lyric and had the melody thing going on. Initially, we played it straightforward, like a rock'n'roll thing, and it was lumpy, it wasn't right. We shifted it around, we tried something else and I think it was Alan O'Duffy, who produced *The Táin* album, he had been working with a band that was a breakaway from 'The Small Faces' and he said, 'The drummer in that (band) would often do a rhythm on the hi-hat. And, of course, 'Shaft'. So he said, 'D'you wanna try that?' Now, essentially it seemed bog-simple, and then you just go 'four-to-the-floor' and it was something that, years later, would have been regarded as a disco beat. But this was ahead of disco. And it just seemed to absolutely nail it and just get the number so tight, and the riff just propelled over the top of it.

In *Tall Tales*, the drummer recalled:

> I knew straight away that the riff was so strong that it had to be a central part of the album's narrative and therefore, probably had to be about Cu Chulainn. We felt it should be vaguely superhero-ish, through which you would define a character. What is he? Who is he? There was a great anti-hero in the Marvel comics called Doctor Doom, who was the nemesis of the Fantastic Four. And then there was this 'Dearg' being red, being Ulster's

bloodied red hand, so it fell together as 'Dearg Doom – The Red Destroyer – and it just seemed to stick. It had a cabalistic resonance.

It's not just Fean's bluesy, distorted reinterpretation riff that makes 'Dearg Doom' so very, *very* good. Carr's lyrics are as strong as the accompanying music is memorable: 'My love is colder than black marble by the sea', 'I am the flash of silver in the sun', and 'I'm a boy who was born blind to pain' being just three examples. O'Connor's gruff vocal style carries the power of the words with ease.

There is a magnificent groove throughout, funky in places, drivingly rocky in others, and the whole song powers along with a tremendous sense of *elan*. Kudos is also due to Devlin for his fabulously funky bass line, which gives the track so much lift and heft. The celebratory-sounding backing vocals are excellent and the instrumental dual between the electric guitar and uilleann pipes (1.32 – 1.48) is wonderful.

Perhaps the most glorious part of the song is contained in its last thirty seconds; here, the key changes from D minor to E minor, and the riff is played on tin whistle, banjo and uilleann pipes. It is fantastic, and it's just a shame that this fades away so quickly.

'Ferdia's Song' (2.44)

The 'Setanta' riff makes another appearance as the introduction to this power ballad; the conversations between Cu Chulainn and Ferdia are set against a largely acoustic backing, as Cu Chulainn tries and fails to persuade his friend from a battle that he knows will end in the other's death. The reference to his 'silver spear' in the final verse relates to 'Gae Bolga', the name of Cu Chulainn's supernatural weapon with which he will kill Ferdia.

The verse chord progression mirrors that of the 'Setanta' riff and it works well in both settings; the sequence itself is unusual (C major, B minor, Bb major, F major), which is extended in the verses to include C major, E minor, A minor, G major, F major, and finally a return to C major. The vocal lines are neatly enhanced by counterpoint melodies on the flute.

The final lyric of the second and fourth verses, 'But Ferdia just laughed, and shook his silver spear and fell to battle again', summons the 'Setanta' theme again. After the final verse, the music grows in intensity, with an electric violin moving to the front of the mix, supported by occasional swells on the organ. The riff changes key upwards twice; from the original key of C major through D major to E major, as the fight between the two friends continues. O'Connor's playing becomes more intense as the rest of the band fade away, leaving the violin in isolation.

'Gae Bolga' (1.12)

This is a reprise of 'Setanta' but with added urgency and drama as the tortured violin mimic's Ferdia's death cries against some distorted guitar triplets. In the background, the swirling organ and bass drum stabs create a chaotic atmosphere that gradually fades to nothing as Ferdia dies.

'Cu Chulainn's Lament' (3.02)

Carr said:

> We had to cram a lot of narrative detail into some of the songs. The lyrics for 'Cu Chulainn's Lament' were from a poem I'd written called 'Love's Lament', which was about suicide. It's as dark as Nick Cave ever was. The trick was that, whilst we were dealing with mythology, I needed to make these words seem personal.

Lockhart supplied much of the music, remembering that 'it was originally my setting of Stevie Smith's poem 'Not Waving, But Drowning". The sound of a howling wind and a church organ playing isolated phrases sets the melancholy mood of this superb ballad. The lyrical vocal is matched in unison by the flute, and, again, Carr's lyrics are superb: 'You felt the chill of midnight ice as I broke your heart in two. And I felt the kiss of emptiness as I watched your life turn blue'.

The chorus is another exquisite section of music. Here the rest of the band (violin, electric guitar, bass, and drums) join in with some excellent backing harmonised singing: 'Life was a game, now I miss your name, your golden hair. No more in your eyes is the blue of skies, only shame'.

A lengthy instrumental section (1.53 – 3.02) has subtle, spacious contributions from electric guitar, violin and flute all working together to create a beguiling atmosphere. This concludes with a reprise of the church organ motif, the music fading again as the next song is introduced on electric mandolin ...

'Faster Than the Hound' (5.37)

Lyrically, this song is from the perspective of Mac Roth, Maeve's messenger, and offers up his view on the events in the story, the 'Hound' being Cu Chulainn, and his savagery.

Initially the song (written by Devlin) does suggest 'Dear Prudence' by The Beatles (from their 1968 release commonly referred to as *The White Album*) with its descending arpeggio pattern, and similar tempo. Here the opening sequence is played, not on guitar, but on electric mandolin.

The longest track on the album, 'Faster Than the Hound' is a stunningly beautiful, restrained, and intricately arranged ballad. Sustained church organ, gentle bass and drums, and well-placed guitar fills support Devlin's sensitive, higher-pitched vocals. Backing harmonies join in for the evocative chorus: 'I saw the stars crash without a sound. Stars go crashing, faster than the hound'.

In the second verse, the line 'I alone knew why' is echoed by an uncredited female voice (according to O'Duffy it is Kay Davis) before another exceptional chorus: 'I saw the ravens, black without a sound, ravens swirling, faster than the hound'. At 2.44, there is an excellent, controlled, distorted guitar solo which, whilst containing plenty of blues stylings, never loses sight of melody, and concludes with a gorgeous sounding, high-pitched bend.

The bridge section (3.22 – 4.15) moves the music in a new direction with the curious addition of a 'Jew's Harp', strummed acoustic guitar, a counter electric guitar melody and more first-class vocal harmonies: 'I travel Ireland in a day. You just nod, I'm on my way. I've got silver wings upon my feet, I seldom touch the ground. The only thing I'm not is faster than the hound'.

The final verse and chorus follow a repeat of the introduction and the song comes to a slow, graceful end which, given the track's constant hypnotic tempo and rhythm, is slightly unusual. 'Faster Than the Hound' is a song where a fade would seem more appropriate and effective.

'The Silver Spear' (2.00)

The first track which sounds like it could easily have featured on *Happy to Meet...*, 'The Silver Spear' (a musical backdrop whilst the men of Ulster prepare their weapons) is a joyously upbeat collection of three traditional tunes.

'The Silver Spear' itself opens proceedings, and the combination of country-style acoustic guitar, bass drum and off-beat hi-hat, and violin melody create a ceilidh feel. Keyboards join in with chordal support and, at 49 seconds, the music segues into 'Tie the Bonnet'. Here the resonances of *Happy to Meet...* are even stronger. This is a considerably more rocky section with overdriven electric guitar, bass, and busier drums really upping the energy levels.

At 1.24, the third tune, 'Crowleys' appears with banjo, and tin whistle joining the violin. This has a similar level of abandon as the coda section of 'Dearg Doom' and, again, finishes too quickly. This is another track where an elongated fade would have been an interesting option.

'More Than You Can Chew' (3.12)

Carr's opinion that the original text of *The Táin* is 'quite witty in places, and a bit far-fetched' is given full rein in his lyrics to this poppy-sounding, major key-based song. Based upon the traditional tune, 'The March of the King of Laois', the words are sung from Cu Chulainn's perspective as he issues a warning to Maeve.

'More Than You Can Chew' bounces happily along for its entire duration. The uilleann pipe melody is a recurring highlight, especially in the instrumental section (1.17 – 1.58), where the electric guitar plays along in unison with a distorted tone, which provides a perfect blend of the traditional and modern sounds.

O'Connor's vocals are joined by the voices of Kay Davis and Jo Collins: 'But before you hit off, let me say that you've bit off, this time you've bit off more than you can chew'. At the same point in the second verse, we have the lines

'Though things may look doubtful, you've got yourself a mouthful, oh, you sure got a mouthful, more than you can chew'. You can almost hear the smile in the singers' voices; this may have been a section which required several 'takes'.

The third verse has the rhythm section dropping out, and the Jew's Harp makes a further, brief reappearance alongside the pipe melody. Multiple vocal harmonies and the returning rhythm section drive this song into a fading coda, with the pipe and electric guitar melody riding high in the mix.

'The Morrigan's Dream' (3.25)

The album's final instrumental, 'The Morrigan's Dream', is another finely crafted piece based around the traditional tune 'Old Noll's Jig'. A preface to the coming battle, the track begins, appropriately enough, with a military drum rhythm to which plenty of reverberation adds atmosphere. Organ, acoustic and bass guitars play a simple chord progression which will underscore the second section of the piece and the traditional tune begins 20 seconds in. This is played with vigour on the violin, with drum fills maintaining the foreboding atmosphere. Keyboards and bass add to the texture, with the church organ appearing for the second section of the tune.

At 1.10, Lockhart takes centre stage, showcasing an organ solo with the main violin tune returning at 1.23, but with even more muscle. Bass and drums are stronger here as the music intensifies before swinging back into the more relaxed second melody. The organ melody is imitated and developed by the violin (1.54 – 2.15) over a sustained keyboard backing. At 2.16, the first melody appears again, followed by the alternative tune where Fean's acoustic guitar gets some heavy strumming action. At 2.56, the feel becomes more relaxed as the 'Lockhart melody' is reprised on violin with keyboard backing, and at 3.10, the music shifts key from F to G major, segueing into…

'Time to Kill!' (5.01)

The first Horslips song to feature Fean on lead vocals, 'Time To Kill!' takes its melodic basis from the hop jig, 'The Humours of Whiskey'. This part of the story is the battle where, as prophesied by the Morrigan, the Connaught army is defeated.

Opening with a slow, a-cappella version of the chorus, followed by a gong crescendo, the central riff on electric guitar and keyboard then takes hold. The busy drum patterns moves from left to right stereo channels and back again, and the punchy verse begins: 'I see the last black swan fly past the sun, I wish I too were gone, back home again'.

The band takes off in the instrumental section, which precedes the chorus, full of energy and spirit and, after a second set of verses and chorus, the electric mandolin solo (2.10 – 2.36) is excellent. Guitar and keyboards briefly take over the celebratory-sounding chorus melody again before the pace slackens and the a-cappella introduction is repeated, this time with a single, sustained keyboard note. Three pairs of huge, booming drums (heavily treated with studio effects) act as a brief prelude to the all-out heavy rock of the track's closing section.

The first pair of verses is reprised (with added studio effects applied to the backing vocals) and the repeated choruses are very busy. The track climaxes with a riotous mandolin solo, another chorus, and a rising progression in the bass over the main melody on guitar and keyboards. Phased drums add to the climax, the song finally coming to rest with an almighty power chord, and more gong.

Except it isn't quite the end. After a short pause there is a strange 'of its time' brief backwards version of the a cappella chorus. Carr described what happened:

> Someone had edited a piece of tape backwards onto the end of 'Time To Kill!' by accident. It was a naked piece of harmony vocal that now, peculiarly, sounded like weird poltergeist language. We were just listening to a playback at Olympic. It sounded so eerie that, in terms of radio drama, it just seemed to suggest some sort of conclusion.

This happy accident does provide a neat end to the album, maintaining the mythological and unsettling mood. In the same way that 'Setanta' pulled the curtain aside, the past now disappears again, in another strange, disconcerting way.

Dancehall Sweethearts (1974)

Personnel:
Eamon Carr: drums, bodhran, percussion
Barry Devlin: bass, vocals
John Fean: guitar, banjo, vocals
Jim Lockhart: keyboards, flute, tin whistle, vocals
Charles O'Connor: fiddle, mandolin, concertina, vocals
Recorded at Rockfield Studios, Monmouth, Wales
Mixed at Kingsway Recorders
Produced by David Fryer
Engineered by David Fryer and George Sloan
Assistant Engineer: Paul Watkins
All tracks composed/arranged by Carr, Devlin, Fean, O'Connor, and Lockhart
Released on 27 September 1974
Issued on Oats Records in Ireland (M007), RCA Records in the UK (APL 1-0709), and RCA CPL 1-0709 in USA

In January 1974, Horslips appeared on *The Old Grey Whistle Test*, a BBC television programme devoted to the emerging rock music scene, performing both 'Dearg Doom', and 'Faster Than the Hound'. Following the release of *The Táin,* a UK tour was undertaken, and in the February, the band recorded a session for *BBC Radio One*'s 'Top Gear' radio programme in London, playing 'The Silver Spear', 'Charolais', 'The March', and 'You Can't Fool the Beast'. Also in February, 'Dearg Doom' and 'More Than You Can Chew' were remixed by David 'Fritz' Fryer for release in Germany as a single, where it went to number one in the charts. Fryer recalled:

> After Alan O'Duffy completed his work on *The Táin* the band wanted to remix some tracks for singles and my name was mentioned. They were so pleased with my results that they asked me if I'd like to produce the next album. I'd recently had my first major success with a version of Neil Young's 'After The Gold Rush' by Prelude, which put me in good stead at the time, because I think Horslips were big Neil Young fans and really liked that version.

The remixed 'Dearg Doom' (but not, strangely, 'More Than You Can Chew') later appeared on *Tracks From The Vaults*. Fryer won out in the remixing competition against Tom Dowd. Both producers had been asked to submit song remixes, and the band chose the versions which they thought best encapsulated their sound. Carr elucidated:

> The results were interesting. There was nothing wrong with Tom's mixes, but they were too smooth to represent what we were. In contrast, Fritz's mixes seemed more energetic, and we were wedded to the theory that we

needed to capture that slightly elusive excitement of the live performance. That was a Holy Grail thing for a lot of artists, and it was why bootlegs were all the rage.

In March, Fryer's remix of 'More Than You Can Chew' was released as a single in the UK with 'Faster Than The Hound' as the B-side. The first half of 1974 saw the band touring in Europe, Ireland, United Kingdom and, briefly, Canada.

Over June and July, recording sessions for the band's third album took place at Rockfield Studios, with Fryer acting as producer. 'King of the Fairies' (coupled with 'Phil the Fluter's Rag', another track from *The Vaults)* was released as a single in Ireland on 8 July, and peaked at number seven. On 9 August, 'Nighttown Boy', paired with 'We Bring the Summer With Us', was issued via RCA, becoming a popular play on the pirate radio station 'Radio Luxembourg'. Further promotion came with the release of 'King of the Fairies' / 'Sunburst' on 24 January 1975. Amidst continuing European touring, *Dancehall Sweethearts* finally emerged. Devlin observed:

> We felt that *The Táin* had a very monochrome sound, and that was emphasised by the cover artwork. We wanted to add colour to our next offering, which is where Fritz came in. I loved working with Fritz; he was a lovely guy. But he walked into a room full of fellas who were already fairly set in their ways when what we really needed was someone to kick the shite out of us. Overall though, I think he did well.

The album cover portrayed Horslips as a quintet of hairy rockers. O'Connor detailed the cover design:

> For *Dancehall Sweethearts,* our faces were to be seen on the cover. I wasn't too wild about the prospect of my dirty fingernails and hairy chest being thrust up people's noses, but I went along with it and somehow, I earned the title of 'gay icon' as a result. The pikey cover was intentionally tongue-in-cheek and as far away from the glam rock image as you could get, and yet we thought it was a really cool picture. Ian Finlay, bless him, had to cope with chaos during that photo session. For the back of the album, we got a mirror to put on top of the coffee table and it broke as soon as we put something on it.

Carr also commented on the cover, saying:

> The album title itself was a pun. I mean, the photo on the album sleeve showed us looking pretty sick and weary, and the idea of describing ourselves was a laugh in itself. It could've been a drawing of a dead, blind Irish harper on the cover, but RCA in England were already getting nervous.

A new aspect to the band's sound was the inclusion of brass instruments, arranged by Ray Russell, and played by an (uncredited) Harry Beckett and Henry Louther, a direction which Fryer actively encouraged:

> Horslips understood the need to be commercial, but in doing so, I don't think they ever lost their integrity. There was a confidence in the band that gave them more of a sense of musical adventure and that seemed to peak when we made *Dancehall Sweethearts.* Few ideas ever really shocked me, and when it was suggested to add a brass section to Irish folk-rock music, it didn't exactly grate. They were very intelligent guys, and they knew that everything was a transition to everything else. I think that *Dancehall Sweethearts* was seen as a vehicle for broadening Horslips' appeal and they seemed to embrace the commercial possibilities, and went for it. I was probably very guilty of encouraging them to do that.

Lockhart added a retrospective note of caution:

> I don't think those brass parts worked in the way we thought they would. I think the 'lurch' was wrong. If you give most jazzers a straight piece to play they will automatically dot it, but what we needed them to play on 'Nighttown Boy' was for them to play it exactly as it was written out. It wasn't ever the case that we gradually drifted into being a rock band. We were constantly experimenting and considered ourselves to be mainstream, but with Irish influences, that were sometimes more upfront. *Dancehall Sweethearts* may have started with the O'Carolan theme, but we curbed its dominance. Motifs ebbed and flowed and 'Nighttown Boy' demonstrated our aim to become more ballsy.
>
> Fritz wasn't trying to drag us into a sonic area that we didn't think was suitable. It was quite the reverse. We overruled him on occasion if we felt strongly about some elements. In some instances, we probably overloaded the arrangements, and Fritz didn't want that because it would complicate the mix. So I point the finger inwardly.

Whilst presented as ten separate songs without any of the tracks segueing into one another, *Dancehall Sweethearts* was still conceptual in approach, although to a much lesser extent than *The Táin*. The album documented the seventeenth-century blind harpist and composer Turlough O'Carolan (1670 – 1738). A native of County Meath, it was O'Carolan's gift for composition, as well as his considerable talents as a musician, that brought him fame. Having lost his sight in his late teens, he began his travels around Ireland. Carr saw similarities between O'Carolan's past and Horslips' present:

> *Dancehall Sweethearts* was something of a road album. There were parallels to be drawn between the rock'n'roll lifestyle we were leading and

> someone like the womanising O'Carolan, who'd collapse into bog holes. We used to laugh and say, 'If he could see us now!' So on that album, it was easier to just rattle off a set of tunes. To follow *The Táin* with an equally conceptual album might have led to a narrow view of what we were about. We didn't want to be seen doing the same thing twice, so if some of the songs suggested using brass, strings or a choir. Then this was seen as an opportunity.

Whatever *Danceball Sweethearts* is, it most certainly isn't *'The Táin 2'*. The overall sound is certainly brighter than its predecessor, and this is a combination of Fryer's production skills, the use of brass instruments, and the greater inclusion of female backing singers. The absence of links between songs gives it a more 'standard' rock album feel, and whilst the travelling musician motif is well juxtaposed between the past and present, there isn't a sense that the listener has to learn anything more about O'Carolan to appreciate the music. And the album did serve up three long-time stage favourites in 'Mad Pat', 'Blindman', and the magnificent 'King of the Fairies'. Fryer said:

> After we finished at Rockfield, I mixed the album at Kingsway Recorders in London. I was satisfied with the result; as a third album, it demonstrated that Horslips were a very well-rounded band.

Let's see, shall we?

'Nighttown Boy' (5.06)

As an opening track, 'Nighttown Boy' is underwhelming. There is nothing wrong with the song *per se,* it's a decent enough four-to-the-floor stomper which chugs along pleasantly enough, but it lacks sufficient drama, energy, or character to engage or maintain the attention.

The cleaner production sound is present and correct right from the start, with a distorted guitar riff, a solid, workmanlike drum rhythm, some tinkling electric piano, and a pumping bass. There is virtually none of the atmospheric reverb which dominated some of *The Táin*, this is a much more direct, 'live' sounding effort.

Then the brass players make their first appearance, and it's divisive. Hats off for trying something new and trying to keep clear of any musical ruts. But equally, hats back on for making such a 'left-field' choice as an opening track. Fans eager to hear a continuation of 'Celtic Rock' were surprised. Well, at least, this one was.

O'Connor's vocals are harmonised by Devlin, with the female backing singers joining for the chorus, and the overall sound is far more akin to the west coast of America than that of Ireland. As if to emphasise this point, the album sleeve stated:

Believe it or not, these tracks have traditional airs concealed about their person.

Sometimes this *is* difficult to believe. For 'Nighttown Boy', this is 'Bill Harte's Favourite'. The traditional source material is extremely well hidden, the only real similarity being the underlying chord progression. The first hint of the 'true' Horslips sound is found in the lengthy, distorted, and at times, manic electric violin solo (2.26 – 3.27). Fean solos for twelve bars, where his phrases have to do battle for sonic space with the brass. It's overly busy, and lacks the musical 'room' around the various instruments, which made the instrumental sections on *The Táin* such a success. Written between *The Táin* and June 1974. there's some good moments in 'Nighttown Boy'; the harmonised guitars work well in the bridge sections (2.03 – 2.23, and again between 3.47 and 4.07). O'Connor gives good voice to some evocative lyrics; 'Silver keys are in my hand, they open doors to worlds that you won't understand' and 'Nighttown Boys can slip and slide on graceful feet'. However, the fact that the track never featured on any official live recording speaks volumes. All in all, it's ...okay. But okay isn't good enough for a song to open the follow-up to *The Táin*.

'The Blind Can't Lead the Blind' (5.16)

Second song, second innovation. Firmly filed in the 'Expect The Unexpected' drawer, 'The Blind Can't Lead the Blind' opens with a delicate choral arrangement of the eighteenth-century Scottish Gaelic song 'Fhir a'Bhata' ('The Boatman'). The choir, 'The Young Dublin Singers', were shipped over alongside their choirmaster for the recording sessions, with Lockhart writing the vocal arrangement.

The original lyric of 'Fhir a'Bhata' (by Sine NicFhionnlaigh) is written from a woman's viewpoint. She is hoping her partner will return when the boats come back to shore. This contrasts with Carr's words which start out referencing O'Carolan ('I don't like being left alone when I'm travelling on the road. I meet too many old ghosts, souls without a home') and then expands over three further verses to deal with loss and leaving. With the reappearances of the choir, these two stories are effectively intertwined.

The excellent counterpoint between the choral singing and the sustained keyboard tone leads into some understated electric guitar arpeggios and a steady rhythmic bass and drum backing. Devlin's relaxed vocals are joined by a lovely counter melody from the violin for the second verse. Lyrically, the third verse is Carr's best work here: 'Well you can move to Boston, take a job in a small hotel. But that won't be the answer you'll still hear St Patrick's Bell'. At this point (2.17) the choral version of 'Fhir a'Bhata' reappears.

An instrumental begins at 2.47, where the music goes into double time for two bars, before reverting to the original feel for four bars. This is repeated and leads into a beautiful section where the violin duets with itself over the verse chord progression. The fourth verse and chorus (3.29 – 4.04) again combines the choir with some bleak lyrics: 'Although the ledge on which you stand is not wide enough for two, there's a blindman at the window and he wants to get to you. When he asks for your direction, you say 'Down, but never mind, I've found a line that I can trust, the blind can't lead the blind''.

The remainder of this impressive song is a repeat of the instrumental section with the electric guitar taking a prominent role with some overdriven lead work and massive slabs of distorted power chords. In the background, the choir, keyboards, and rhythm section enhance the powerful play-out rather than smother the sound, as the music gradually fades away.

'Stars' (4.59)

A cheerfully upbeat double-tracked guitar and bass duet leads into this engaging pop-rocker, written by Devlin. The verse lyrics are at odds with the chugging, major key composition and the very melodic vocal line: 'Half of my lifetime, spun between dance and light. Easy connections lost in the cold twilight. Clutching the powers that remain, searching them for ways to turn them to gain, I wrestle the Devil alone, and turn confused to find I'm lost in the air'. Words and music mesh more effectively in the upbeat chorus: 'Then, as we danced, all the stars fell in the sea'. The female backing singers add much to the thrice-repeated line. After the second verse and chorus, Fean lets loose with some blisteringly, bluesy phrases featuring an impressive climbing pentatonic run as its centrepiece.

Disappointingly, the third verse is a reprise of the first, but the repeating chorus has a clever arrangement to it: 3.29 – just vocals and drums; 3.42 – an arpeggiated keyboard line is added together with handclaps, and at 3.48 the full instrumentation with plenty of added percussion leads into the fade.

Good song though 'Stars' is, it sounds too 'American'. Whilst it has obvious commercial appeal, especially with its addictive chorus, there's something lacking in the instrumentation; some prominent violin, banjo, tin whistle, or uilleann pipes would have redressed this substantially and pulled the track back across the Atlantic.

'We Bring the Summer With Us' (2.28)

Based upon the traditional song 'Thugamar Fein an Samhradh Linn' ('We Brought The Summer With Us'), this short instrumental keeps the original's melody line but goes to town on the arrangement. Title tenses aside, this is a wonderful example of maintaining the traditional whilst simultaneously channelling the music through a modern medium and arrangement.

A distant, sustained synthesiser plays the tune without accompaniment at first. As the melody is repeated, a secondary keyboard tone provides a chordal backing. accompaniment. At 0.37, a third synth joins the texture playing a bouncy counter melody in the bass moving between stereo channels, and the music pauses slightly to draw breath at 0.51.

The melody is then passed to the concertina as O'Connor, Devlin, and Lockhart play a descending Baroque-style chord sequence. The texture changes with the disappearance of the second synth pattern. At 1.30, the music reaches a climax with crashing cymbals indicating the final section of the arrangement as the mood turns temporarily melodramatic.

At 1.37, the piece really takes flight as overdriven guitar, keyboards, bass, and a bodhran all join the melee. The tune loops around and around, finally going into a celebratory sounding fade.

'Sunburst' (4.34)

Every time I listen to this track the words 'Steely' and 'Dan' leap to mind. 'Sunburst' sounds to me like a distant cousin of 'Show Biz Kids' (from the 1973 album *Countdown To Ecstasy*); the reference points being the near-relentless groove, the electric piano tone, a distorted guitar sound, the female backing singers chorus refrain, and the reappearance of the brass players adding an overly American sheen to the track. Of all the songs on *Danceball Sweethearts*, 'Sunburst' is the one where the 'new' production style seems to have held the most sway. Recalling the bird-in-flight imagery of 'Dearg Doom', Carr's lyrics are again on-point: 'I come down like an eagle, an eagle far from the sea, won't you set me free?' He recalled:

> We arrived for sessions at Rockfield with some material unfinished. I had found that the three-line verse concept fitted one of the emerging songs… A series of linked images weren't sufficient to create a proper song structure, so Barry helpfully contributed a middle section. He also proposed the last triplet; 'You wait for me to take you, and make you a hunter like me when we're flying free', which tidied up the piece by suggesting an ending.

It is Devlin's bridge section (2.18 – 2.48) where the American reins are loosened temporarily, and a poppier feel takes hold, but this is short-lived. A flurry of triplet-based phrases from the brass leads into a more 'Horslipian' sound, with O'Connor's voice adding grit to the lyrics: 'Sun is shining on her wings, keeps her happy, makes her sing. But her talons flash upon the things she needs to keep her smiling. Prey is sighted from above, it's moving fast but not quite fast enough, deathly grip, cruel love, take me to your sunburst'. A rising, big band-style brass fill appears, and we are back in the 'Dan-Groove'.

The song's final verse has the main vocals intertwined with the backing singers, with the coda reprising the opening lines. Distorted guitar, male backing vocals (of the verse lyrics), and female singers ('Want to feel your sunburst') build the intensity as the track rides off into the sunset. No violins, mandolins, or concertinas were harmed in the recording of this song.

And so ends what was, in old money, Side One. And, at best, it's…fine. There are no *poor* songs, and it is clear that the band were keen to expand both their musical and commercial horizons. However, if a listener new to the band was to be recommended any Horslips album (thus far), *Danceball Sweethearts* wouldn't be it. The relative absence of the traditional Celtic instrumentation leaves a hole which is not adequately filled by the new textures or ideas. Fortunately, Side Two proves to be better. *Much* better...

'Mad Pat' (6.08)

O'Connor's electric mandolin arpeggios fade in, and it's his vocals that relay the tale of 'the country fiddler, a jester, a riddler, a joker, a singer of songs.' Acoustic guitar, bass and drums join for the pre-chorus, with a crescendo on the organ bringing in the powerful chorus. It is at this point that the traditional jig 'How Much Has She Got?' is tucked away; the line 'Mad Pat's gone back on the road, a wire string fiddle is his only load...' bears similarities to the source material.

The second verse follows a similar sonic pattern, with the chorus again including some impressive organ playing to good effect. An interlude featuring the mandolin, melodic bass lines, and a clever use of guitar harmonics ushers in a full-on rock instrumental section. Distorted slabs of guitar power-chords follow a Black Sabbath-style doomy descent over which Fean plays an overdriven, tasteful, blues-based solo. At 3.41, O'Connor takes over 'lead' duties with a deftly executed, highly melodic mandolin solo, and at 4.10, the quieter, arpeggiated introduction returns. The final verse is, sadly, a retread of the first verse. The final chorus is further fleshed out with backing vocals, and the song gradually disappears with a mixture of mandolin, bass, and guitar harmonics.

'Mad Pat' is a welcome return to *The Táin* levels of composition, invention, and arrangement. The fact that the song would be a mainstay of tours, and feature both on *Live* and *Live at the O2,* as well as being treated to a quieter, more acoustic focused rendition on *Roll Back*, all point to its longevity and justified 'classic' status amongst fans. 'Mad Pat' is essential Horslips; a unique blend of traditional melody, lyrical inspiration, an excellent arrangement, and classy performance places it in the top drawer of songs by the band. Where it is joined by...

'Blindman' (3.31)

'Blindman' had originally been written for inclusion on *The Táin.* Carr explained the song's history:

> Unsure of how best to tell the Táin story, I overwrote, and much of the stuff quickly became redundant as the narrative jigsaw pieces slotted together. 'Blindman' went into the live set almost as soon as it was written and remained there. The Blindman (in Yeats' 'The Death of Cu Chulainn') had been in Maeve's tent and the scarecrow, my pun on the Morrigan, was his Fool. The 'Late Late Show' verse was probably a device to briefly represent the present, but it may just have hinted at something dark.

In many ways a companion piece to 'Mad Pat' ('Blindman' would follow it in live performances), the pair enjoy several similarities. Fean's carefully picked, double-tracked arpeggio introduction, O'Connor's rough-edged vocals, the power-chord stabs, and similar medium tempo all fit both tracks.

The lyrics are exceptional; 'Do you ever feel like dancing, when the evening turns to gold? Or does life's simple melody make your blood run cold?', and 'Blindman, halfway there, empty as a nun, tears turn into diamonds at the eclipse of the sun' being just two examples.

The interplay and arrangement of the instrumentation is impressive throughout. Fean turns in another distorted solo (2.15 – 2.58) and the final verse brings this excellent composition to a powerful end. Another 'instant classic', the track's only fault is that it isn't long enough. An extension to the instrumental section, or a play-out featuring violin or uilleann pipes would make the song even better.

'King of the Fairies' (3.31)

The album's *piece de resistance,* and a track to rival 'Dearg Doom' as another magnificent example of 'Celtic Rock', 'King of the Fairies' is the best track on the album. Carr commented:

> The bass drum is four-to-the-floor and with the snare, I settled on something that had a pile-driving feel, playing on the first beat of each bar instead of the (conventional) second. It was a million miles away from what was expected from 'folk-rock' at the time.

Fean detailed the band's arrangement:

> 'King of the Fairies' was well known to most of us, because it was a popular tune you'd learn in music lessons at school. Our idea was to place it in a rock format. It was a given that people would know the tune, in Ireland at least, and so we had a head start. Charles' fiddle part was a fairly straight reading of the original tune and I added the guitar solo and banjo section, but we experimented quite a bit with the beat and Jimmy's use of the Moog synth.

Chugging overdriven guitar and double-tracked Mini Moog synth open proceedings. Hi-hat and bubbling bass join in, and O'Connor's violin plays the melody 'Bonny Charlie' which dates from the Jacobite era. Fean changes the mood with a distorted, blues-tinged guitar solo (1.21 – 1.52) before switching to a creamier tone for the second half of the melody in unison with a lower octave version on the synth.

At 2.08, O'Connor takes over, and there's some brief rhythmic humour when the groove is replaced by a triplet feel (2.12 – 2.17), before the four-to-the-floor feel is restored.

The texture changes again at 2.24, where Lockhart's tin whistle skills are on display, quickly joined by Fean on banjo playing the melody in unison. Violin is added into the mix. At 2.55, there is a modulation from E minor up to A minor, followed by another at 3.03 down to G minor, returning to A minor at 3.11, at which point the track steams to a tight end.

Fryer said:

> I thought that 'King of the Fairies' was a tremendous victory for contemporary folk music. All my acquired rock'n'roll skills as a producer were out in force to achieve the rawest possible sounds. For me, it remains one of the most powerful examples of Horslips' abilities to fuse musical genres.

'Lonely Hearts' (5.31)

Written by Fean, 'Lonely Hearts' returns to the 'rock band on the road' theme, and is the most musically ambitious track on the album. It's a brisk and energetic number powered along by hi-hat and busy bass lines, with harmonised vocals delivering the sober reality of the rock'n'roll dream: 'Neon spells out my name, but I enter from the alley outside. All the faces I can see think they own a piece of me there are times when I just want to hide.'

The pace and mood slacken at 1.36 with some soulful, introspective vocals over a simple guitar, keyboard and bass backing with atmospheric cymbal swells: 'Sometimes I sit and ask myself 'Where is it going to end?' I sit and wonder what keeps me going, keeps me happy when I'm travelling round'.

At 2.30, a rising chord sequence is punctured by power-chord stabs from bass and drums, with the violin and flute mirroring the guitar melody. This moves quickly into a reprise of the introduction, and another bluesy, distorted guitar solo. Lockhart's organ swells in the background as this frenetic sequence builds to a further reprise of the introduction, before landing on the final set of lyrics, the best of which is: 'Though my face is on the posters and my name is in the charts, my only claim to fame is I look like easy game to a million lonely hearts.' At 4.50, the music modulates from G minor to A minor with another anguished-sounding solo from Fean as the song goes into a fade.

'The Best Years of My Life' (1.48)

Based upon 'Saint Anna's Polka' (also known as 'Saint Anna's Reel') but taken at a much slower pace, 'The Best Years of My Life' is the album's only real ballad. It's a straightforward piece; two verses and a chorus, followed by a further two verses and another chorus to end, making it the shortest song on the album, and a peaceful coda to the wide selection of vibrant music which has preceded it.

Lyrically, this song fuses the O'Carolan (for the first verses) and rock band themes (for the second set), although these are also interchangeable.

The chorus ('The best years of my life were spent in Barrowlands and Borderlands, The best years of my life were spent in Galway') is simple, and the entire song feels like a hymn. Organ dominates the accompaniment, with the flute providing a melodic interlude after the first chorus. Electric piano arpeggios are added for the second set of verses, and violin joins in the interlude preceding the second chorus.

'The Best Years of My Life' is a curiosity, a 'take-it-or-leave-it' experience which is very much a showcase for Lockhart's talents. There's nothing *wrong* with it, and there are, again, some telling lyrics: 'And the ones who came to cheer me, why they hardly knew, I'd play for those who'd hear me, if you want I'll play for you'. It does, however, remain a track that, once heard, doesn't demand to be listened to again.

The Unfortunate Cup of Tea! (1975)

Personnel:
Eamon Carr: drums, bodhran, percussion
Barry Devlin: bass, vocals
John Fean: guitar, banjo, vocals
Jim Lockhart: keyboards, flute, tin whistle, uilleann pipes
Charles O'Connor: fiddle, mandolin, concertina, vocals
Recorded and mixed at Rockfield Studios, Monmouth, Wales
Produced and engineered by David Fryer
All tracks composed/arranged by Carr, Devlin, Fean, O'Connor, and Lockhart
Released on 11 April 1975
Issued on Oats Records in Ireland (M008), RCA SF8432 (UK), and RCA CPL 1-1068 in USA

Following the release of *Dancehall Sweethearts,* Horslips toured the United Kingdom and Ireland in the autumn of 1974, and in November, they played in Canada for four weeks, then crossing into the United States. In January 1975, RCA Records released 'King of the Fairies' / 'Sunburst' as a single, and by the end of April, recording for the new album was finished at Rockfield Studios, again with Fryer producing. The songs which would appear on *The Unfortunate Cup of Tea!* were mainly written in a rented cottage in Puckane, County Tipperary, and the band's fourth album is their first disappointment. Fean said:

> We didn't give ourselves enough time after the previous album to write new material and make a wise selection. *The Unfortunate Cup of Tea!* was our attempt at a pop album, but it was made when we were at a low ebb. No one seemed particularly interested in making it and for the first time, recording felt like a chore. It was just a collection of songs with one or two good moments, like 'The Snakes Farewell To The Emerald Isle', but generally, I'd say it remains the least inspiring of all our albums.

Devlin concurred but added a more positive retrospective take on the album:

> The album was lambasted by the critics and there was good reason. But in revisiting it more recently, I found that there was actually some really interesting stuff going on. 'Turn Your Face to the Wall', 'Ring-a-Rosey', 'Everything Will Be Alright', and 'Flirting in the Shadows' are nice songs played well.
>
> We were too stressed out. It was our most 'unfinished' effort and it certainly lacks the 'big song' that other albums had. Some of the tunes were to some extent, doodles that needed more attention. It was probably frustrating to Fritz (Fryer) that he never had the time to impose a moral authority on the band. Given a different set of circumstances, we could have

made a seriously good record with him, because he knew his stuff, but we never got that opportunity. Hindsight defines what is or isn't a good album, or perhaps sales, and we always did our best at the time. *The Unfortunate Cup of Tea!* is the album that divides our fans. Some hate it, while others can't see what all the fuss is about.

This fan neither hates nor loves it. When it's good, it's very good indeed. However, these moments are relatively few and far between. My overriding impression of the album is one of frustrated disappointment. There is some good material present, and the usual excellent musicianship, but these factors are outweighed by some mediocre compositions, and a production style which largely fails to ignite either heart or mind. Lockhart pinpointed the probable reason for the relative failure of the project:

We'd usually take a fortnight off, rent a cottage and get the new songs written and rehearsed in advance of recording so that we didn't waste expensive studio time. We ran a very tight operation, financially speaking, so the rule was never to leave it to the last minute to write new material. *The Unfortunate Cup of Tea!* was the most obvious exception to this rule, and what the album really lacked was road-testing prior to the recording. I can't think of a single song from that album that was played live before we went to Rockfield.

Fryer's opinion on what was to be his last album with the band was:

I accepted that our relationship would have its natural span. I got the impression that they wanted to take the traditional elements of their music as far as they could, from album to album. Having seen the treadmill of their daily touring routine, I knew they were working so hard it was knocking the spark out of them. They never had the chance to recover, either creatively or spiritually, to take a step back and see where they were going. On reflection, I think *The Unfortunate Cup of Tea!* was aptly named.

If the overall impression of the songs on the album is dispiriting, the cover is anything but. O'Connor takes up the story:

I used to collect 3D stereoscopic cards from all manner of sources in Ireland. I had a series called something like 'Irish Villagers' or 'Scenes From An Irish Life' showing things like women knitting, and one of the cards depicted a lad courting a girl. There was a cup of tea on the table and an open window. We decided, after succumbing to the effects of too much tea, to use this very folksy image for the album and it was Eamon's idea. We used to rummage through the O'Neill book and look at daft titles of tunes. *The Unfortunate Cup of Tea!* was one of the more wonderfully bizarre titles that we found and it just stuck. While it was a great image, it still lacked something. The front room window was dying to have something happening in it ... like shoving a green monster through it from the other side by the band, maybe? That was my daft idea.

The two cottages we were renting in Puckane ahead of the sessions looked quite similar to the house in the stereoscopic card, and so we had a photo of us taken for the back cover. We stuck Robbie McGrath in a green body suit and he didn't like it one bit. The suit kept his head in place, so we had something to work with at the artwork stage. We didn't have the luxury of Photoshop, but we did have Geoff Halpin who ended up working for Hipgnosis. He was a master of this kind of thing and also came up with the lettering, while Tom Griffin drew the monster and cup illustrations.

The back cover is the scene from outside the cottage; O'Connor is on lookout duties, whilst Fean, Lockhart and Devlin are holding the monster up to the window. Carr is watching with his back to the wall and a concerned expression on his face. This 'Victorian drawing room scandal meets silent movie via Spike Milligan' motif (to quote Devlin) continues on the liner sleeve of the album where the following appears:

Historical Note; Down through the ages, the quest for *The Unfortunate Cup of Tea!* has stirred the imagination of poet and pauper alike. Now with the discovery of the '24th Track' we can begin to grasp its potent symbolism and, hopefully, chart its course from ritual to romance, with a bullet. This is a mixed metaphor, but it can be played on mono reproducers provided either a compatible or stereo cartridge wired for mono is fitted. Or you could use an oxymoron.

The reference to the '24th Track' is a nod to Rockfield Studios, where the recording desk had recently been upgraded. Unfortunately, the humour and spark present in the cover design is rarely matched by the songs themselves. There is the welcome return of a stronger element of traditional instrumentation, and the absence of the brass players means *The Unfortunate Cup of Tea!* has a more 'Horslip-ian' sound. However, the production is at times too boomy, the dry clarity of *Danceball Sweethearts* is missing, and in its place, reverberation is excessively applied to most of the instruments most of the time. Unfortunately, some of the songs are just not good enough and lack the melodic gift and instrumental invention that has been the hallmarks of the preceding albums. Only two of the tracks come in under the five-minute mark, and in the main, the others give the impression of stretching themselves too thin.

RCA released a truncated version of '(If That's What You Want) That's What You Get' backed with 'The Snakes' Farewell to the Emerald Isle' as a single on 13 July 1975 in the UK.

Abandoning the concept of the 'concept album' is a good way of keeping yourself fresh, and of avoiding criticism as 'one trick ponies'. But with *The Unfortunate Cup of Tea!* this attempt at a poppier style does the band few favours. This is the first Horslips album I remember being underwhelmed by. It sounded more mainstream, less progressive, uninventive, and very light in the fusion department. Sadly, over time my opinion has changed little, and *The Unfortunate Cup of Tea!* remains the only Horslips studio release where the album title is better than most of its contents. Excepting, of course, the absolute nadir that is *Short Stories,Tall Tales* but we'll get to that in a while.

'(If That's What You Want) That's What You Get' (7.10)
The longest track on the album is also the lengthiest song they ever recorded in a studio. I'm not against extended songs at all, but to succeed, they need to go places, develop themes, and expand creatively to fill the time available. This one doesn't. At all.

There's a solid, driving drum rhythm and a funky, American feel to the guitar. Fiddle, more guitar, and flute, then introduce the main instrumental melody, and we're into Fean's vocals 38 seconds in. So far, so sprightly. However, Carr's usual sharply focused lyrical gifts here sound hackneyed; 'Well, here's a surprise, I can see it in your eyes', and 'Well you're my desire. You can set my soul on fire' being just two egregious examples.

A single bar of 2/4 time in amongst the relentless 4/4 beat appears just before, and 'trips' us into, the full-blooded chorus, which ends with the vaguely memorable refrain 'I'm crying, but that won't change a thing. For crying will never change a thing.' The sound is enhanced by some (uncredited) female backing singers; presumably, the same ladies who contributed to *Dancehall Sweethearts*. Their presence underscores the American feel of the song; soulful, funky, and pulsing. A neat roll around the tom-toms ushers in the second instrumental introduction, verse, and chorus.

There then follows a lengthy instrumental section (3.29 – 4.29) which is an extension of the introduction with an added bluesy guitar solo. What really robs the song of its proper impact is the amount of time spent in and around the tonic key (D minor). Out of its seven-minute plus duration, over four and a half minutes features the introductory section in various unremarkable forms. After a while, attention starts to wander and only momentarily returns for the third chorus.

We are now past the five-minute mark with orchestral strings and the backing singers beginning to swamp the sound. If the intention was to go for the long, grooving, epic opener then sadly, only the first criteria has been fulfilled. There's a thin line between a groove and a rut and by this time, the band were firmly stuck in the latter. The track could have ended at this point and been slightly the better for it. However, on it rolls with another verse (the opening lines 'You can make me happy anyway you want to, if you want to' make an uninspired reappearance) and chorus, but very little by way of variation to what has been before is heard. The song goes into a long fade and, sadly, it's not the best seven minutes of your life. Regrettably, this sets the tone and style for much of what follows ...

'Ring-a-Rosey' (4.35)

This track starts promisingly with an atmospheric acoustic guitar and keyboard chord sequence. Then the rhythm kicks in with the electric mandolin taking the melodic lead over a very similar sounding groove and tempo to the previous track. This highlights another issue with Fryer's production decisions for the album; Carr's drums are recorded 'dry' and placed forward in the mix. Other instruments have, on occasion, varying degrees of reverberation applied to their sound and the effect is, in the main, unbalancing.

The lyrics, sung by Devlin, are better here: 'Like an angel crying mercy to a storm, you call from shadows where you don't belong. And the candle that I carry in my dark, was once a torch to love that I held back'. The music is drivingly melodic, but veers into a commercial vein as it builds to a crescendo for the chorus, with some nice harmonised flute lines in the background.

The second verse occupies identical musical territory, although, again, the lyrics are more involving than the music: 'As you walked across the meadows towards the moon, made the midnight stranger welcome much too soon'. In the chorus, some classy backing vocals add to the atmosphere, and a two-bar concertina phrase moves us into the bridge section.

Here the lyrics and music diverge further. Given the associations of the symptoms of the plague with the nursery rhyme song title, this section is disconcerting. The underlying chord sequence and vocal melody travel further into pop territory. The concertina provides a melodic counterpoint line throughout this section, and Fean steps forward for a trademark bluesy, overdriven guitar solo (2.43 – 3.09). In the background, mandolin and piano are supported by a prominent bass and drum sound.

Verse three contains some evocative lyrics and some predictable rhymes: 'In my sleep, I see a carnival of ice, you're wearing white and pirouette so nice. When I stop to ask the nature of surprise, a veil of contradiction is slipped before my eyes'. The final chorus (replete with flutes and layers of backing vocals) leads into the coda, where the mandolin is played through a wah-wah pedal. The instrumentation disappears, leaving the acoustic guitar and keyboards replaying the introduction.

This is a neat touch, however, this sequence clashes with the guitar and bass introduction to the next song. The closing chord sequence for 'Ring-a-Rosey' is a repeated E major and A minor sequence; the opening for 'Flirting in the Shadows' is E minor followed by A minor. It would have been far more effective to have a proper linking passage between the two numbers to give a smooth transition, rather than the clumsy effect which we have here. If it was a deliberate ploy to set a sinister atmosphere, as suggested by the title it could have been better executed. As it stands, the transition is jarring and just doesn't work.

'Flirting in the Shadows' (5.43)

Another example of a reasonable idea stretched out for too long, 'Flirting in the Shadows' is a slow-moving, atmospheric song with plenty of interesting instrumental touches, but not a lot else going for it.

Sustained slide guitar, electric mandolin with wah-wah pedal enhancements, moody bass lines, subtle electric piano phrasing, and restrained, occasionally militaristic drumming all play their parts effectively. However, O'Connor's rough-edged vocal tone doesn't suit the song as well as Devlin's would have done.

The best parts of the song are the lyrics ('... a girl who has no smile, her long hair may look careless, but those dark eyes beguile', and '...a girl who cannot sleep, tossing stones in midnight pools, discover these pools are deep'), and the bridge section (2.13 – 2.36). Here the music builds in power with some more good lines: 'We worked so hard to build a dam that would stem the dreams of a desperate man...'.

There is an effective instrumental section (2.36 – 3.16), but by now, we've heard the mandolin enough already. A change to a violin would have worked comparative wonders here. Fean's tasteful electric guitar playing resolutely remains a highlight of the song throughout.

An unnecessary reprise of the bridge section leads into the final verse, where there is an amusing, brief 'Sci-Fi' synth sound effect after the line 'Perhaps she's passed this way before' (4.32). There's a further minute of familiar instrumentation as the song eventually goes into a fade, once again dominated by the wah-wah mandolin.

'Flirting in the Shadows' would receive a shorter, faster, and much better interpretation on *Roll Back*, but that would take decades to emerge.

'Self Defence' (6.08)

The softly played guitar arpeggio introduction to 'Self Defence' is *very* reminiscent of 'Blindman'. Fean's sound is subtly altered by the use of tremolo on the repeated phrase. Some light percussion and a sustained organ add further colour before a heavy drum fill drives the song into a reverb-drenched, strongly funky groove, driven by relentless hi-hat semiquavers.

The chorus is the strongest vocal element of what will turn out to be one of the album's more 'proggy' tracks; 'Now I can't tell wrong from right, can't tell black from white, seems to me they're one and the same' with Devlin singing at the higher end of his range. The dynamics drop down for a reprise of the introduction, a second verse and chorus. So far, so similar to much of what has gone before.

A reversed cymbal crescendo (racing from the left to right stereo channel) ushers in the instrumental section. At 2.03, the energy level changes dramatically, with a descending chord sequence being joined by some heavy, double-time drums as the music gathers intensity and volume, leading into a spectacularly manic flute solo over the verse chord sequence. A syncopated climbing chord progression (2.55 – 3.04) indicates a possible return to a vocal section, but instead this has Lockhart happily off the leash for a further twelve bars. The climbing chord progression returns, this time leading into a repeat of the chorus.

At 3.37, the 2/4 time feel returns along with the guitar chord progression which began the instrumental, this being played four times before the final verse where full voice is given to the lyrics, which conclude with 'Colour blind, I can't tell if you're blushing or angry or blue. I can't decide if it's angel or demon that's rough-riding you'. Another chorus is followed by an eight-bar reprise of the instrumental, where Fean throws in some typical, bluesy lines.

The final verse has Devlin at the top of his range; 'Can't attack, you're a killer, but you got me hypnotised. Can't look back, you could turn me to stone, you got heavy eyes'. A final chorus (with impressive backing vocals) leads into an energetic play-out where keyboards and then the wah-wah'd mandolin provide the instrumental highlights.

'Self Defence', when it gets going, acts as some form of reassurance to confused fans who may have been wondering exactly what had happened to the band by this point. There is energy, invention, and melody powered along by a robustly rocking rhythm section. It's the best song on what was side one and lifted hopes that this quality level would be maintained. Sadly it was not to be …

'High Volume Love' (5.30)

Before 'High Volume Love' begins there is some 'Goons-style' nonsense in the form of the courting couple from the album cover being interrupted by the appearance of the growling monster, with some pseudo-dramatic piano as an amusing accompaniment. It's the most involving part of the track. Carr takes up the story:

> The chatter and the noises you hear…are just us having a laugh late one night. That's Jim as the husband and myself as the wife at the start of the song, believe it or not. We were worn out, make no mistake, but our humour was intact, as indeed it always was, even in the darkest of situations.

Then, 16 seconds in, it's 'set the controls for the heart of the familiar'; a chugging rhythm, a steady tempo, plenty of reverb, and another unfulfilling side-opener. 'High Volume Love' has moments of similarity to Thin Lizzy with the harmonised guitar lines.

The verse lyrics are nothing special ('And then I saw her dressed in silk, leaning back on velvet she was white as milk', anyone?), and whilst the female singers enhance the poppy chorus, 'High Volume Love' remains four-square and predictable throughout. Once you've heard the first verse and chorus, you have, in effect, heard the second and third combinations as well.

The near-total absence of traditional instrumentation doesn't help, and Fean's creamy-smooth distorted solo (2.50 – 3.44) again raids the Lizzy vault for ideas from 3.32 onwards. The third verse does at least benefit from some harmony whistles in the background, and the backing vocalists add class to the final chorus, but really I'm scratching around for diamonds in the dust here. The song ends as it begins, fading away into welcome obscurity.

'The Unfortunate Cup of Tea!' (1.14)

A brief, dramatic, piano introduction (think Rachmaninoff or Tchaikovsky in their wilder moments) heralds in a *very* welcome return to the spirit of *Happy to Meet...* Also known as 'An Cupan Tae', this traditional reel is given a music-hall style makeover. The violin takes the melody with some percussion in the background alongside the steady 'um-cha' (bass/treble) piano accompaniment. A tin whistle joins in as the sound effects of an Irish pub near closing time appear. All this fun, alas, ends all too soon ...

'Turn Your Face to the Wall' (6.28)

As you were then? No, not at all! 'Turn Your Face to the Wall' is the second of the three really good songs on the album.

Guitar and mandolin set up a catchy major key-based sequence to which bass and drums add significant rhythmic heft, and then a lovely, haunting melody from uilleann pipe and flute melody appears. The beat is deceptive here; there are five bars of 2/4 time followed by a single bar of 3/4. This sequence is repeated before the introduction finishes with three more bars of 2/4 time. This is the band back to their best, joining the old and the new, and creating something both impressive and original as a result. It's a very welcome addition to the album!

O'Connor's vocals work well over the solid 2/4 time signature, which goes into double time for the second half of the verse. The introduction returns in a slightly truncated form before a second verse. At 2.13, the chorus appears and it's a thing of some magnificence, with added atmosphere from the uilleann pipes.

Some gentle keyboards lead into a reprise of the second introduction, and then the music just *explodes* at 3.03 with thunderous drumming, surging organ, gritty lead guitar, and a driving bass. Finally, the band has rediscovered their mojo, for this is tremendous stuff. At 3.27, the melody is decorated with bluesy guitar fills, and the feel goes into double time for a joyful 33 further seconds. Here again, there is some clever beat displacement; there are nine bars of 4/4 time before a single bar of 2/4. Three further bars of 4/4 are followed by another single 2/4 bar and the section finishes with a further pair of 2/4 bars. When analysed like this, it sounds complex. In listening reality it's just *really good music*.

At 3.51, the *sturm und drang* section is reprised, but only for eight bars and then the instrumental reins are handed over to O'Connor, who turns in a highly melodic violin solo, which is more country than Celtic in feel, played over the verse chord sequence.

Another chorus, replete with uilleann pipes and the gentle keyboard link, leads into the introduction again and the final verse and chorus. At its climax, O'Connor's voice rises in pitch and the *sturm und drang* section is repeated, this time with a wah-wah pedal enhanced guitar solo. The music comes to a chaotic end with feedback, and a rasping violin, segueing neatly into the next track.

'Turn Your Face to the Wall' is, finally, (for this album) proof that Horslips had still 'got it'. All their uniquely identifiable and important attributes are here, resulting in an excellent song with plenty of changes in texture and dynamics, some genuinely heavy rock energy, and a strong vocal melody. It's stirring stuff, and this listener's spirits are lifted up…

'The Snakes' Farewell to the Emerald Isle' (5.30)

…and down again. 'The Snakes' Farewell to the Emerald Isle' is a sparse, moody instrumental which, like so much before it, stretches its limited, although enjoyable, themes too far and too thin for too long.

Opening with a rain-stick approximating a snake's hiss, the title, a random suggestion by Carr, is a reference to the myth that St. Patrick banished snakes from Ireland. This is, of course, a fallacy, and is more likely to refer to his determination to rid Ireland of its pagan traditions.

The best part of the track is the gorgeous, sustained guitar tone Fean achieves. With a straightforward drum rhythm, a(nother) steady tempo, and plenty of reverb, the bass (also played by Fean), rhythm, and lead guitar all sound suitably evocative and hypnotic. For this two-minute opening section, the overall mood is about as far removed from Ireland as can be imagined. The sustained tone and phrasing is reminiscent of Carlos Santana's fusion of blues with South American rhythms and his own band.

At 2.05, the flute takes over, introducing a new melody ('Ard Ti Cuan') over the unrelenting chord sequence (D minor, E minor, D minor, and A minor) as Fean adds some blues fills in the background. At 3.35, the guitar melody returns, with some occasional flute harmony and counter-point lines. However, by now, 'The Snakes' Farewell…' is starting to sound like both a very protracted goodbye and an extended 'jam session'. Rather than going into the expected fade, the band reprise the short link, which handed solo duties back to Fean as a coda. The sound of some flowing water and birdsong segue into the final song …

'Everything Will Be Alright' (5.19)

...and some twinkling keyboard arpeggios, alternating between D7 and G7, which is joined by organ, guitar and Devlin's first lines: ' You won't let me see your daughter, make her turn her back on me.' The rhythm section kicks in for the rest of the verse and builds to a rousing chorus repeating, 'Everything will be alright'. A sparkling, short section of church organ and guitar chords follows, which will form the underlying chord sequence for the forthcoming instrumental section.

The second verse has Carr back on form: 'You won't let me build a spire, reach out to the sky. You cut me from my living god, can't see him till I die. You won't even let me learn, I dream but cannot write, I often hear a song in dreams, singing 'Everything will be alright''.

The bridge is equally impressive, featuring a new chord progression and vocal melody: 'I bought a gun from a soldier on the run, just to teach a thing or two. But I threw it back, took up my harp, tried to make my dreams come true.' This leads into the short organ and guitar section before the third verse and chorus: 'You try to cut me from the land, old men move out to die. Your shadow moves across the sun, soon poets start to lie. But theirs will always be a song of smiles that bring the light. The man behind the dark can hear me ... saying 'Everything will be alright'.'

At 2.22, a new instrumental section begins with portentous chord changes (D major and F major) being repeated until a violin solo (2.39 – 3.07) which develops into a fantastic, but too short, rendition of the traditional tune, 'The Trip to Durrow'. Following this, the fourth verse is, regrettably, a retread of the second rather than a fresh set of lyrics. The song builds to a climax with added strings in the mix behind the thrice repeated 'Everything will be alright'. 'The Trip to Durrow' makes a welcome reappearance, and the guitar emerges with some excellent phrasing, then the band fade away, leaving just the strings and traditional instruments playing 'The Trip to Durrow'. First, the strings fade, then the banjo and tin whistle also disappear.

By 4.48, the track appears to be over. But there's more! The banjo and whistle fade back in briefly and then out again. What wags! It was the mid-1970s; there was a lot of this sort of thing about back then.

'Everything Will Be Alright' is an excellent final song, again marrying a melodic rock song with traditional Celtic elements to produce something unique and memorable. If more of the rest of *The Unfortunate Cup of Tea!* was up to this standard, then the album could have been something special. As it is, there are enough flashes of inspiration to make it a worthy listen on occasion but, with the exception of *Short Stories, Tall Tales*, this is the Horslips album that I play the least. Mostly underwhelming, occasionally overwhelmingly good, the mean feeling for album number four is one of being merely whelmed. I just wish it were otherwise.

Drive the Cold Winter Away (1975)

Personnel:
Eamon Carr: bodrahn, Arabian bongo
Barry Devlin: bass
John Fean: fiddle, mandolin, banjo, and guitars
Jim Lockhart: harpsichord, celeste, table organ, pipe organ, piano, Uileann pipes, flute, tin whistle, recorder, vocals
Charles O'Connor: mandolin, fiddle, concertina, Northumbrian pipes, vocals
Recorded at Trend Studios
Engineer: Fred Meijer
All tracks arranged by Carr, Devlin, Fean, O'Connor, and Lockhart
Released on 6 November 1975
Issued on Horslips Records (MOO9) Ireland

Following the release of *The Unfortunate Cup of Tea!*, Horslips continued to tour in Ireland, England, and Germany. In July, RCA released a new single: '(If That's What You Want) That's What You Get' / 'High Volume Love'. In October, Denny resigned as the band's manager and this, combined with RCA's decision not to renew the band's contract, should have dented their confidence. Instead, they used the opportunity to regroup, with Jim Slye taking over as manager. Slye's role was restricted to the band's Ireland operations; elsewhere, Lockhart acted as tour manager.

Following the declining sales curve the band had endured since the early highpoint of *The Táin,* Horslips were treading water in close proximity to some sort of limbo. O'Connor summarised the situation:

> We retreated to take stock and were in no-man's land for a while, falling back on our own resources and seriously evaluating our plans.

Carr explained the *raison d'etre* for *Drive the Cold Winter Away*:

> We had done our own releases in Ireland and we had the set-up for it, so we thought we should avail ourselves of this opportunity. We'd always talked about doing a nice little acoustic album, so what was to stop us? There were a few seasonal songs and the idea was, 'Why don't we do a (Phil) Spector? Why don't we do a Christmas album? We had a lovely tune, 'Drive the Cold Winter Away', and named the album after it.

The album was completed in just four days (*four days!*) during September and was available for purchase two months later. With the absence of any electric instrumentation, beyond Devlin's bass, this shone a new light on the band. The title track was, in O'Connor's words, 'an odd choice', not because it was a drinking song but more due to its associations with the Cromwellian period of influence in Ireland. He continued:

> We needed to make an album quickly, so Jimmy and I researched a pile of tunes together with a winter theme. I was keen to include some Northumbrian references on that album, such as 'The Snow That Melts the Soonest' and 'Thompsons'. The sessions were very refreshing, because we'd never worked that quickly or economically before.

Lockhart continued:

> It was an album we had talked about doing for a long time, but it wasn't the kind of thing we felt was an acceptable move in the first few years of our studio career, because we were focusing on the harder-edged stuff. So we all enjoyed the process of going back and discovering some of these old tunes that we had kind of ear-marked. It was a side of Horslips that only a few people had actually heard.
>
> Charles and I put the basic idea together within a couple of weeks. Then presented everything to the band for their reaction and made the album in four days at Trend Studios, reuniting with our old eccentric Dutch engineer Fred Meijer.
>
> *Drive the Cold Winter Away* probably saved our bacon at that point in time, because it earned us a few quid and we approached it with a low-cost, cottage-industry mentality; the album served a good purpose. It got us back to our roots and it was fun to make, but more than anything, we bought some time for ourselves by putting it out, because we were already writing material for our next album.

The band's humour manifests itself on the album cover. O'Connor takes up the story:

> The image on the *Drive the Cold Winter Away* cover was an old engraving from a source book of Victorian pictures. Meanwhile, on the back, we had a montage of Sessiagh Lake, where we rehearsed with a photograph I'd taken of the mountain in the background and the New York skyline planted on it. We were represented by characters I found on old postcards. Johnny, Eamon, and Barry were portrayed as dancing girls, Jim as a piper and myself as Mickey Mouse. I loved all that kitsch. That's why we had the ornamental shamrock garland framing the front cover. And the 'To' and 'From' on the back was a sweet little send-off. I'm actually very fond of that cover and the album itself. I was forming ideas for the cover design in my head over our four days in the studio.

This light-hearted approach is also evident in the personnel information. Devlin, in addition to playing the bass, 'grumbled a lot'. Lockhart's 'bewildering' array of instruments is referred to as 'Octopus City', whilst Carr's list of percussion is followed by an in-joke: 'Derek Taylor was not in

the studio'. In addition, each track has a brief commentary on its provenance. I have added these quotations before each track review to give additional perspective. The album notes conclude with the following:

> This is a stereo album we've wanted to do for four years. It can be played on mono reproducers or on Christmas Day; or both. Happy Christmas.

Drive the Cold Winter Away is a charming diversion. Stripped right back to their acoustic origins, the strength of the tunes is in their arrangements and variety. Of the thirteen tracks, only five feature vocals (six if you count the final seconds of 'Drive the Cold Winter Away'). There is sometimes a danger with music drawn from a very specific genre; after a while, the tracks can seem to blend into one another. This is not the case here; clever choices of tunes and intelligent arrangements mean the collection is consistently varied and entertaining.

Of course, it would be fascinating to hear *Drive the Cold Winter Away* being given the 'proper' Horslips treatment with drums, overdriven guitar, and electric violin and mandolins adding fresh interpretations to the old melodies, but this was not the intention here. Consequently, the album presents Horslips in a new (old) light. It shows that, despite the apparent drift away from their roots which *Danceball Sweethearts* had suggested, and *The Unfortunate Cup of Tea!* had continued, they remained enamoured with the traditional music of their collective upbringings.

Drive the Cold Winter Away represents the end of the first era of Horslips; a frenetic period which saw the band establish themselves as a force to be reckoned with, but with diminishing returns in terms of album sales. The workload of writing, recording, and touring looked like it would burn them out, and so this project represented a pause, and a change in their work ethic, before they unleashed the masterpiece of their second era.

'Rug Muire Mac Do Dhia' ('Mary Bore a Son to God') (1.49)

> We start off with a medieval arrangement of 'Rug Muire Mac Do Dhia', a traditional carol with Celtic words.

'Rug Muire Mac Do Dhia' is one of only a few carols in Irish, the lyrics being taken from the poem 'Prattling Clerics' written in 1578 by Owen O'Duffy (no relation).

Sustained keyboard notes and Lockhart's distinctive vocals open proceedings, his melody mirrored by the keyboard. The vocal line is then echoed on violin, with bass and tambourine adding to the texture. A second verse in an identical style follows. For the third verse, the violin joins in with the vocal melody. At 1.22, the sound becomes stronger; the acoustic guitar is more to the fore, and the bass gains greater prominence. The fourth verse is sung by multiple voices, the song coming to a quick end. There is a processional feel to this track, exemplified by the 2/4 time signature and steady tempo, supported by the assorted percussion.

'Sir Festus Burke' / 'Carolan's Frolic' (3.38)

> 'Sir Festus Burke' is a celebratory Carolan tune. We've joined it here to the festive 'Planxty Tom Judge', which you may know as 'Carolan's Frolic'.

A bright harpsichord rendition with added mandolin, 'Sir Festus Burke' is a happy mixture of Baroque and traditional Irish stylings. Banjo is heard at 0.31, with acoustic guitar and violin being added to the mix at 1.02. At 2.16, the texture changes as the tin whistle summons in 'Carolan's Frolic' accompanied by a rhythmic bodhran backing. Acoustic guitar is added to the sound at 2.30, and at 2.55, the instrumentation changes to guitar and mandolin, with tin whistle and bodhran rejoining for the final section of this joyful medley.

'The Snow That Melts the Soonest' (4.26)

> 'The Snow That Melts the Soonest' was picked up from a Newcastle street singer in 1821 and brought over by Charles in 1971. We're not sure what happened in-between!

The album's first ballad opens with a lovely mixture of piano and acoustic guitar arpeggios over which a mandolin riff travels from the right to the left channel. The violin takes up the main melody joined by a simple bass accompaniment.

O'Connor's vocals are beautifully phrased, with the harpsichord joining the accompaniment for the second verse. The violin instrumental after the second verse follows the vocal melody line, and the third verse maintains the existing mood. The second half of the fourth verse sees the instruments drop out, leaving just violin and bodhran, with the band rejoining for the title refrain. A further violin instrumental acts as a coda to this lovely song, with the mandolin swooping left and right again as the music draws to a close.

'The Piper in the Meadow Straying' (2.34)

> We found the fine hornpipe 'The Piper in the Meadow Straying' in Johnny Fean's repertoire. We're not sure if whoever wrote it had just heard 'Deck the Halls' or vice versa, but it's a nice Christmassy tune.

A rousing double-tracked violin and acoustic guitar instrumental is enhanced by the subtle presence of a celeste. Whilst there are some melodic similarities to 'Deck the Halls', especially in the third phrase (bars 17 – 20 inclusive), the arrangement does not dwell on these. At 1.30, the tune is transferred to flute and celeste, although it is just possible to hear the other instruments playing faintly in the background. Violin and guitar rejoin at 1.45 for the coda of the track.

'Drive the Cold Winter Away' (2.29)

> Playford's 'Dancing Master' of 1651 is the official source for 'Drive the Cold Winter Away', but we first heard it from Jimmy, who claims he unearthed it single-handed!

Also known as 'All Hayle To The Days', this was originally a seventeenth-century English carol introduced to the band by O'Connor, who knew the tune as a Cromwellian period drinking song.

After a four-bar acoustic guitar introduction, the flute takes the melody for the next sixteen bars, ably supported by steel-strung guitar arpeggios. For the second time through, banjo joins the texture. At 1.17, the style changes from the steadily flowing 6/8 time into a more formal waltz feel (3/4 time), with the violin taking the melody over the guitar and banjo accompaniment.

Sixteen bars later, the arpeggios return with the flute playing the tune alongside the violin. The full ensemble continues with another play-through of the central melody, the track coming to a close with multiple voices singing the song title, as the key changes from D minor to D major for its final chord.

'Thompsons' / 'Cottage in the Grove' (2.38)

> 'Thompsons' and 'Cottage in the Grove' are a pair of reels. The concertina is a perfect match for their delicate cadences.

Another O'Connor import, 'Thompson's' is a joyful, upbeat tune which opens with some fine concertina playing, and a banjo providing an apt chordal backing. At 1.19, the track changes into 'Cottage in the Grove' with tin whistle and banjo sharing the melody along with the concertina over a stout-sounding piano accompaniment. A bodhran adds a powerful rhythm at 1.13 to the combination, which steams along happily to the tune's close.

'Ny Kirree Fo Naghtey' (2.20)

> 'Ny Kirree Fo Naghtey' is a Manx carol. The title is translated as 'The Sheep 'Neath the Snow'. Manx is quite close to both Donegal Irish and Scots Gallic (in Irish the title would read 'Na Caoirigh Faoi Shneachta'), but it was only ever written phonetically, hence the peculiar spelling. The tune is lovely, don't you think?

This has a similar sounding feel to the beginning of 'Drive the Cold Winter Away', with acoustic guitar arpeggios overlaid with a sustained keyboard melody and a simple bass line. Lockhart's vocals are sung in Manx, and the track has a haunting atmosphere, notwithstanding its medium tempo and unchanging instrumentation. A translation of the lyrics would have been useful here. What actually happened to the sheep? Enquiring minds want to know.

'Crabs in the Skillet' (2.15)

> 'Crabs in the Skillet', just the thing for a Christmas starter.

A bouncy, minor key concertina-led tune, 'Crabs in the Skillet' is a fabulous example of the band having plenty of fun with a traditional melody. The tune has three sections to it, each eight bars long, and after the initial 24-bar play-through, acoustic guitar and mandolin join in for the reprise of all three themes.

'Denis O'Connor' (2.46)

> 'Denis O'Connor' is another Carolan tune (this time in celebration of The O'Connors of Belanagare). This was first played on Christmas Day in 1723. It's worn well!

Harpsichord plays the initial themes solely in the right stereo channel, which is then handed over to the concertina on the left. Soft-sounding keyboards provide a pleasing counterpoint which then drops out to be replaced by more harpsichord at 1.30. This arrangement is repeated, with some additional keyboard fills, before the tune comes to its close.

'Do'n Oiche Ud I Mbeithil' (3.30)

> Jimmy did the arrangement of ('That Night in Bethlehem') and it gives an unusual feel to this old Gaelic carol.

An introduction of syncopated acoustic guitar and bass gives 'Do'n Oiche Ud I Mbeithil' a surprisingly blues-rock feel. Some percussion here would have added even more to the texture. The main melody is played on the flute before Lockhart's relaxed vocals, sung in Gaelic, commence. An additional steel-string guitar makes a brief appearance in the mix at 1.17, before the second verse, with the flute repeating the melody as an instrumental section and an extra guitar making more of a contribution. The third verse continues the song's rhythmic yet soothing feel, which fades away as the introductory melody is played a further time.

'Lullaby' (2.23)

> Although we play the 'Lullaby' as an instrumental, it's really a song. The version we have has Victorian words, but there are other versions, other lyrics.

'Lullaby', first documented in Joyce's *Ancient Irish Music* and attributed to Owen Roe O' Sullivan (1748 – 1784) has another excellent instrumental arrangement which grows and flows throughout. Acoustic guitar provides the chordal accompaniment to the flute melody, which is played through twice. 48 seconds in the melody is repeated alongside a harpsichord, with a violin appearing at 1.12. For the third time through the tune, an additional, harmonising flute is added as the track draws to a neat end.

'The Snow and the Frost Are All Over' / 'Paddy Fahey's' (2.48)

> That we're great fans of Irish Céilí bands should be evident from this arrangement!

Opening with a vigorously strummed acoustic guitar, over which the tin whistle plays the main melody, 'The Snow and the Frost Are All Over' is another great, foot-tapping instrumental. The violin takes the melody over after 53 seconds, to which a banjo is added, also playing the tune. In the background some off-beat piano chords are heard as the tune builds into a key change from D minor to G minor at 1.40, and we are into 'Paddy Fahey's'.

Violin and banjo share this tune over acoustic guitar and, latterly, piano, with some interesting percussion playing. The tempo from 'The Snow and the Frost Are All Over' is maintained, the key change giving added impetus. This track is another one guaranteed to make the listener feel good, the sheer exuberance of the playing carrying the music.

'When a Man's in Love' (4.13)

> Charles has been singing 'When a Man's in Love' for so long we decided to get it all over with in one go. This song has been collected as far away as Donegal, Wexford, and even Nova Scotia. How's that for universal appeal?

Mandolin and guitar provide the initial musical backing to O'Connor's tongue-in-cheek rendition of the lyrics, which probably originated in County Antrim. Bass joins for the second half of the first verse in this seven stanza story-song, and there's a fantastic violin phrase played alongside the line 'And softly she undid the latch and slyly I slipped in'. This idea is reprised in the next verse '…oh, take me to your bed.' As if to prove they are not merely cruising through the song, the band show some invention in the arrangement, with

Above: Devlin, Carr, Lockhart, O'Connor, and Fean. Given the fashion of the time, this photo is, mercifully, in black and white.

Below: Fean, O'Connor, Devlin, Lockhart, and Carr decades later. The famed camaraderie remains intact. *(Mark Cunningham)*

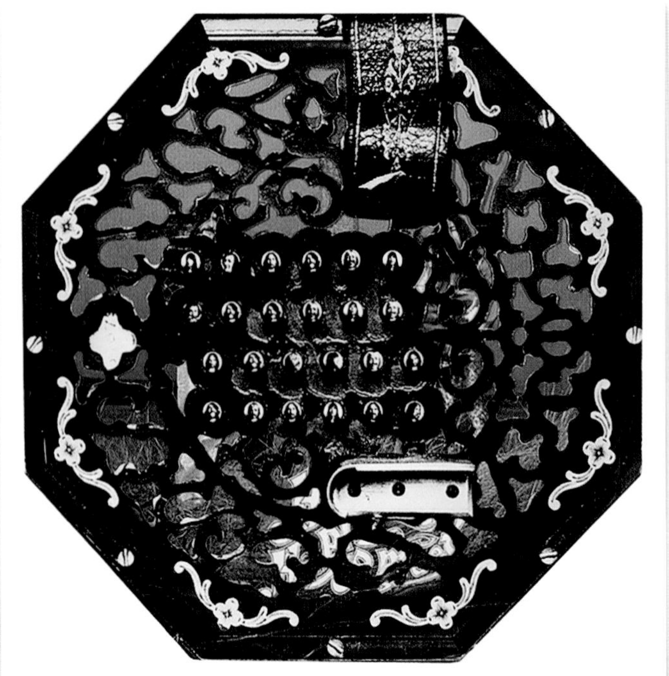

Left: The elaborate cover of *Happy to Meet, Sorry to Part* is as ambitious and adventurous as the music itself. *(Oats Records/RCA/Atco)*

Right: *The Táin* – The band's first conceptual masterpiece. *(Oats Records/RCA/Atco)*

Right: Devlin, Fean, O'Connor, Carr, and Lockhart pose for the cover of album number three whilst waiting for the barbers to open. *(Oats Records/RCA)*

Left: *The Unfortunate Cup of Tea!* is, unfortunately, the first dip in quality. *(Oats Records/RCA)*

Left: The band performing 'Furniture' at the National Stadium, Dublin in 1973.

Right: Devlin and O'Connor during one of the softer sections of 'Furniture'.

Left: Fean and Lockhart; quiet music, loud clothing.

Right: The band playing 'Dearg Doom' on *The Old Grey Whistle Test*.

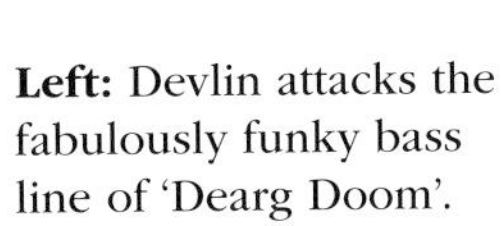

Left: Devlin attacks the fabulously funky bass line of 'Dearg Doom'.

Right: Carr giving his drums some punishment from the same show.

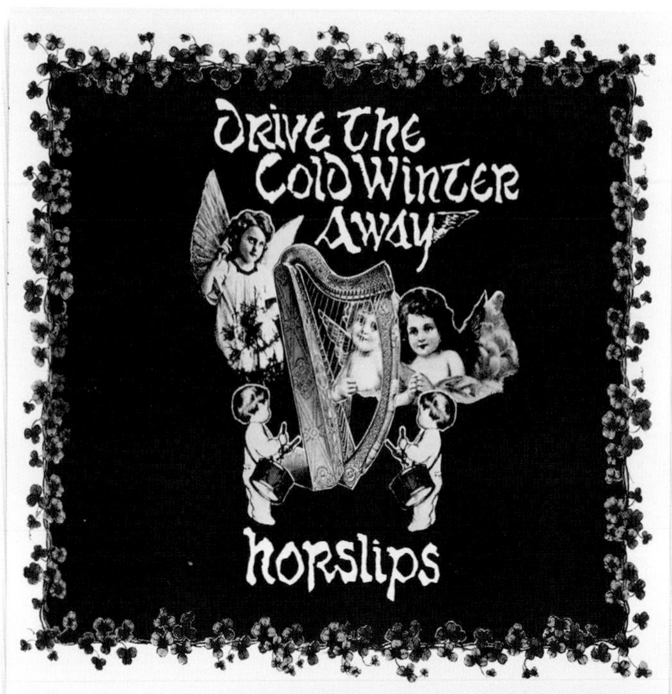

Left: *Drive the Cold Winter Away* – a charming collection of winter-themed, all-acoustic songs and instrumentals. *(Horslips Records)*

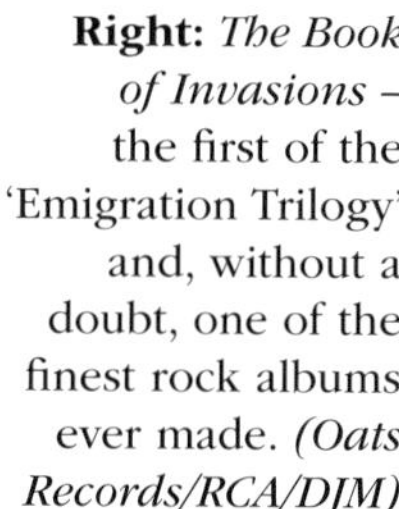

Right: *The Book of Invasions* – the first of the 'Emigration Trilogy' and, without a doubt, one of the finest rock albums ever made. *(Oats Records/RCA/DJM)*

Right: *Tracks from the Vaults* – an intriguing collection of rarities. *(Horslips Records)*

Left: *Aliens* – Volume 2 of the Trilogy is a collection of excellent songs and, of course, exemplary musicianship. *(Oats Records/RCA/DJM)*

Left: In a possible homage to The Beatles playing on top of the Apple Corp building in London in 1969, here Horslips treat Dubliners to 'King of the Fairies'.

Right: The video was shot for John Molloy's Dublin programme.

Left: Johnny Fean; cool guitarist, even cooler temperature!

Right: The band performing 'Blindman' at the National Stadium, Dublin in 1975.

Left: The same song seen from the side of the stage.

Right: O'Connor gives voice to Carr's emotive lyrics.

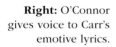

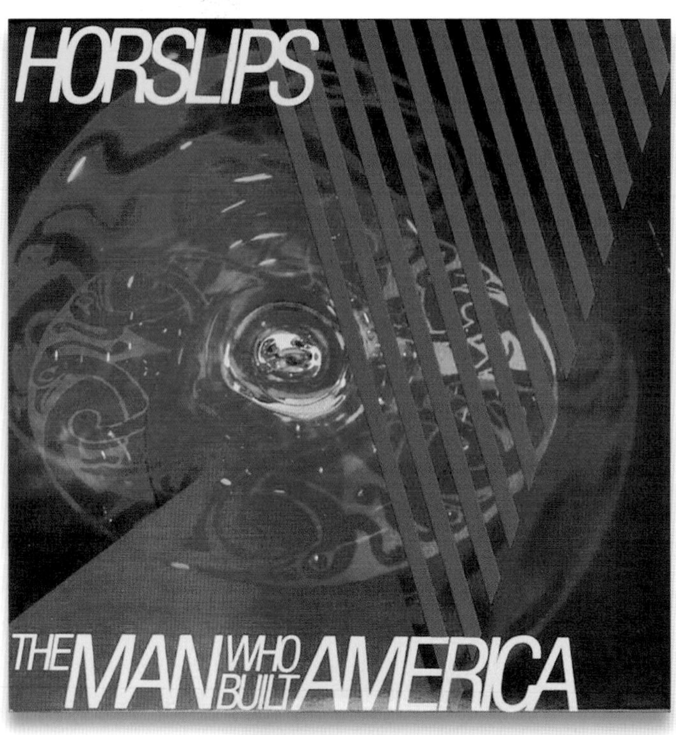

Left: *The Man Who Built America* – the final part of the Trilogy. Some great songs are sabotaged by a production style that moves the band too far away from their unique sound. *(Horslips Records)*

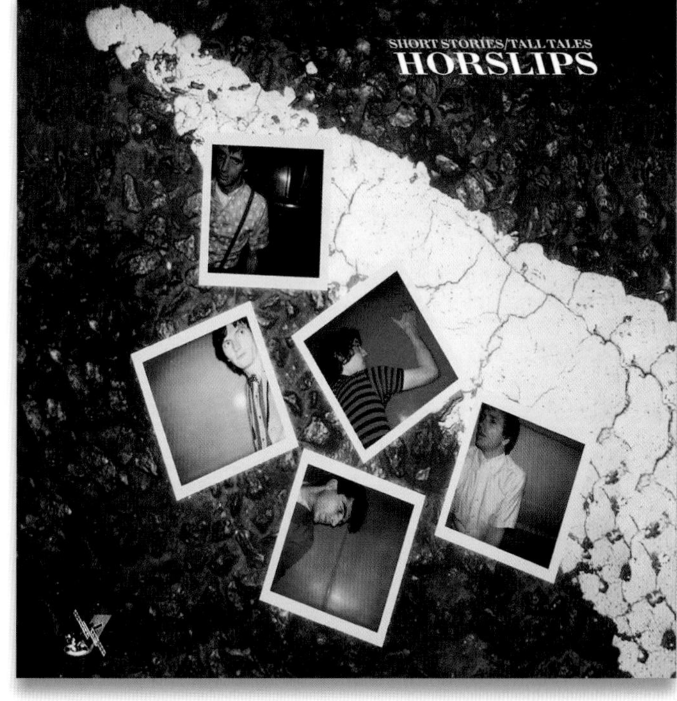

Right: *Short Stories, Tall Tales* – two semi-decent songs and one fabulous acoustic ballad cannot save this album. *(Horslips Records)*

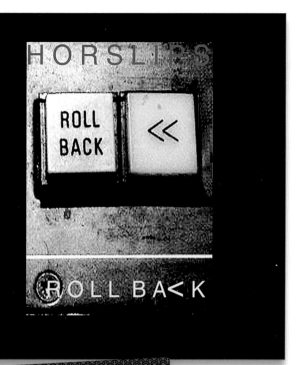

Right: *Roll Back* – a joy to listen to with classic songs getting an acoustic reworking to great effect. *(Horslips Records)*

Left: *More Than You Can Chew* – the mother of all box sets. Part all-encompassing musical history, part doorstop. *(Madfish)*

Left: The band performing 'The High Reel' at the O2 in Dublin in 2009.

Right: Ray Fean steps into Eamon Carr's shoes for the gig.

Left: Just a man playing an electric guitar onstage to thousands of fans.

Right: Horslips perform on Fleadh TV in 2019.

Left: Devlin; either singing or about to crack a joke ...

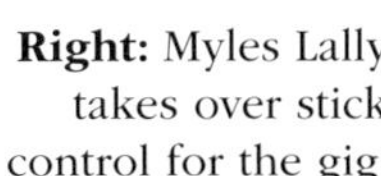

Right: Myles Lally takes over stick control for the gig.

Above: O'Connor and Devlin share a gag during the 'Reunion' era. *(Alamy)*

Right: Devlin in full voice. *(Alamy)*

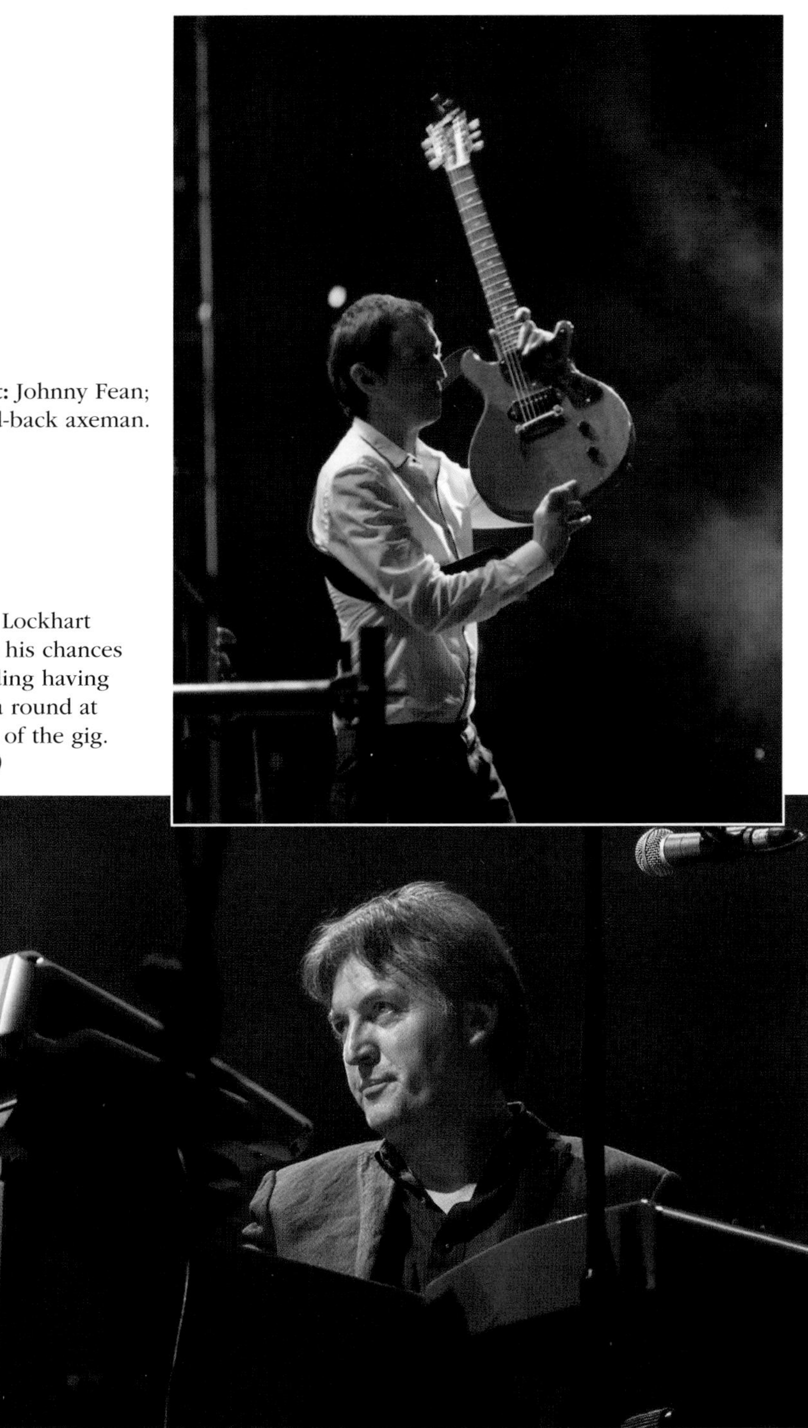

Right: Johnny Fean; the laid-back axeman.

Below: Lockhart eyes up his chances of avoiding having to buy a round at the end of the gig. *(Alamy)*

Above: This guy came up with the riffs for 'Dearg Doom' and 'Sword of Light', amongst many others. Just let that sink in. Riff in peace, Johnny.

syncopated chords sounding under the words 'To take you to my chamber love…' at 1.07.

The violin provides an instrumental interlude, with the bass being surprisingly busy, before the music subsides for the next verses. Flute is added to the next instrumental section, with the syncopated chords making a further brief appearance in the accompaniment. The tale ends appropriately enough for this refreshing album, with the couple getting married, and a short instrumental to round things off.

Live (1976)

Personnel:
Barry Devlin: bass, vocals
John Fean: guitar, vocals
Eamon Carr: drums
Charles O'Connor: fiddle, mandolin, vocals
'Irish' Jim Lockhart: keyboards, flute, tin whistle, vocals
Produced by Harold Burgon
Recorded with Rolling Stones Mobile
Mixed at Trend Studios and at Sound Techniques, London, by Fred 'Cool Vibes' Meijer and Vic Gamm
Released April 1976
Chart placings: Did not chart

Before the release of what this fan considers the band's masterpiece, a double live album – *Live* – appeared on 23 April 1976. Capturing performances over two nights during February 1976 using the Rolling Stones mobile of *Happy to Meet…* fame, *Live* was produced by Harold Burgon, and mixed by Fred Meijer.

Devlin has a dim opinion of the fundraising release:

> …it's the only Horslips album I won't defend. If someone asked me to recommend one of our albums to a potential new Horslips fan, that would be bottom of the list. It sounds like our recording budget was a fiver. The truth is, when you're desperate to make some money to fuel running costs, as we were at that point, a live album is normally the default solution.

Seemingly recorded in a barn with the doors left wide open, the production is dire and sounds as if a single microphone was hung from the rafters whilst Burgon pressed 'Go'. The instrumental blend is unbalanced, the vocals are, at times, almost inaudible, and whilst the crowd reaction is ecstatic, *Live* is hardly an accurate portrayal of the power (and glory) of a Horslips gig. In the liner notes, the band's familiar humour is captured:

> This is a stereo record. That's 'cos we were running all over the stage while we were playing. If in doubt, ask those who were there.

The album cover featured Devlin's shamrock-shaped bass across the front and back of the gatefold sleeve. O'Connor takes up the story:

> We wanted some movement, so Ian Finlay shot it at slow speed as the bass was wiggled about from side to side, hence the out-of-focus, streamed effects. Geoff Halpin also designed the lettering for the album in the style of wires. For the inner gatefold, we added some of Ian Finlay's live

photography of us playing at the Pavilion Cinema in Dun Laoghaire, where the album was recorded.

The tracklisting for *Horslips Live* is:

'Mad Pat', 'Blindman', 'Silver Spear', 'High Reel', 'Stars', 'Hall of Mirrors', 'If That's What You Want (That's What You Get)', 'Self Defence', 'Everything Will Be Alright', 'Rakish Paddy', 'Rakish Paddy' (Continued), 'King of the Fairies', 'Furniture', 'You Can't Fool the Beast', 'More Than You Can Chew', 'Dearg Doom', 'Comb Your Hair and Curl It', 'Johnny's Wedding'

As if to emphasise the slapdash nature of the endeavour, the 'new' track ('Rakish Paddy') faded out at the end of side two, only to re-emerge ('Rakish Paddy' – Continued) as the first track on side three. Except it isn't 'Rakish Paddy' at all; it's 'The Trip to Durrow', which closes side two and re-fades in on the next side, which *then* segues into 'Rakish Paddy'.

Lockhart commented on the album:

> *Horslips Live* sounded pretty lo-fi and didn't capture the magic of our shows at the time. What I do think, however, is that it drew a bold line between two distinct phases in our career. It was like saying, 'That was our past; here's to the future.' And behind the scenes, we were very much working towards our future with an exciting bunch of new material.

The Book of Invasions: A Celtic Symphony (1976)

Personnel:
Eamon Carr: drums, bodhran, percussion
Barry Devlin: bass, vocals
John Fean: guitar, banjo, vocals
Jim Lockhart: keyboards, flute, whistles
Charles O'Connor: fiddle, mandolin, concertina, vocals
Recorded and mixed at Miracle Studios
Produced by Alan O'Duffy and Horslips
Engineered by Alan O'Duffy
Assistant engineer: Robbie McGrath
All tracks composed/arranged by Carr, Devlin, Fean, O'Connor, and Lockhart
Released on 12 November 1976
Issued on Oats Records in Ireland (M0012), RCA in the UK (DJF 20498 – 25 February 1977), and DJM DJLPA-10 (USA – 9 May 1977)

The band continued to tour Ireland, the UK, and Germany, and on 22 July, the first single from the forthcoming album was released. Recorded by Pat Morley at Dublin Sound Studios, 'Daybreak (Excerpt from A Celtic Symphony)' reached number two during a 22-week stay in the Irish chart. The B-side of the single was 'Oisin's Tune'. Both numbers would later turn up on the mid-career retrospective compilation *Tracks From the Vaults*.

The Book of Invasions was produced, once again, by Alan O'Duffy, who later said:

> If I were an arrogant man, I'd say they were wrong to change to a different producer after *The Táin*, as we had a track record of getting it right, we had a good partnership in the studio, but I imagine they wanted to see how the rest of the world made records.

Lockhart viewed the re-engagement of Duffy as part of the return to form, which had begun to dissipate with *Dancehall Sweethearts*:

> It was in discussions with Alan that we started to once again value the diverse palette of musical textures that we had at our disposal. Anyone could have brass and string arrangements, but we had a lot more going for us internally. Where Alan was coming at musically was The Beach Boys and really getting the most from multi-track overdubbing.

Carr concurs with this:

> When it came to figuring out how to approach the sound of *The Book of Invasions*, we realised the best way forward would be to take a direct, logical step from where we were at *The Táin,*as opposed to veering

off into any experimental stuff. We saw what we had, with linking passages and ambitions for counterpoints and harmonies, and the spread of instrumentation. And we recognised that Alan had a very good understanding of all that process, how we arrived at it and how it worked. So we were lucky to get Alan back.

The album was a return to the 'full' concept album, which had served the band so well with *The Táin*. With *The Book of Invasions*, Horslips took the bull (colour unspecified) firmly by the horns for a second time. Carr said:

While *The Táin* was the big saga of Irish mythology, *The Book of Invasions* was about the genesis of the Irish race. We ran shy of it for a while, thinking, 'We couldn't do that, it's outrageous'. But that feeling gave way to 'Aw, fuck it, let's try'. The three-movement idea was perfect for us; it was a symphony waiting to be written.

Lockhart added:

The Book of Invasions benefited from a much longer gestation period than the previous albums, because we weren't being pressured by a major label to get it finished. We were able to relax and enjoy some artistic freedom to let our ideas mature. We all had the material written, meticulously arranged, and well-sequenced before we started to record, and had been playing a lot of it on the road from early 1976.

We talked about the kind of tunes that would fit into the piece, and the feel of the music we should write, and all the songs seemed to flow very quickly. When that came to fruition at Miracle Studios, there was just something about the way everything slotted together so perfectly, and that was a really lovely bit of completion.

Devlin's view was:

We always responded well to having something big to aim for, and that was definitely the case with *The Book of Invasions.* A big piece like that gives a band a common purpose. At the time, there were no individual songwriters amongst us as such; we all tended to bounce ideas off each other. The unifying purpose tended to come from the scale of the writing. We were all capable of writing songs, and if we had a big well of songs to pull from, it would give cohesion to a project.

Whilst the band was turning a creative, near-full circle, O'Connor's distinctive cover artwork remained a constant feature. Similar in tone and mood to the cover of *The Táin*, for the new album a monochrome close-up of his left eye is seen looking upwards. On the back cover, five individual ghostly images of

each member of the band is captured floating against a black background. He explained the inspiration behind the imagery:

> My idea for *The Book of Invasions* cover was heavily influenced by one particular image called 'The Tears', the female subject of which looks like a silent film actress. It was taken in the early thirties by the great avant-garde photographer and painter, Man Ray. I really liked the eye because it was looking up to Heaven and the stars, and I imagined a possible Celtic connection. I emulated that image by asking Evelyn Lunny, a make-up artist at RTE and sister of the famous Donal, to paint my eye silver and flatten my eyebrows for a photo session. I'd already had the idea to cover the cornea of my eye with a Celtic motif at the artwork stage and also to reverse the image for the inner sleeve. At the time, I wanted to print the cover on chrome paper to give a silver effect, but it worked well without it.
>
> On the back of the sleeve, Ian Finlay and I developed this idea of the band's swirling faces. The swirls were done manually with time exposure rather than adding an effect in the processing. We had to sit each member of the band on a chair, give them a 'three, two, one' countdown and get them to move their heads to the left or the right on cue. It took a while for them to relax into it and give us the right effect – Eamon looks particularly demonic – and in the end, we had a really love set of pictures.

With *The Book of Invasions*, Horslips are back to firing on all six cylinders (Alan O'Duffy is hereby promoted to an essential part of the music-making machine). Without a duff track in earshot, and possessing three classics in 'Trouble (With a Capital T)', 'The Power and the Glory', and 'Sword of Light', the entire album is just magnificent. I could go on, and, believe me, I will. But this isn't just my opinion. In September 1976, Angus McKinnon, writing in the *New Musical Express* concluded:

> Son-Of-Táin this isn't. *The Book of Invasions* is more ambitious, sophisticated, and ultimately more substantial than its forerunner.

***The Sunday Times* commented:**

> The music is a magical, muscular mixture of percussion, fiddle, guitar, mandolin, concertina, voices. In beauty, coherence and invention, a rare success.

Two decades later writing a retrospective review for *Mojo* magazine, Colin Harper opined;

> *Invasions* still sparkles with more hooks than a shepherd's convention, and in containing perennial anthems like 'Sword of Light' and 'Trouble (With a Capital T)' is simply essential.

So, what's it all about, then? The sleeve notes lay out a brief history of its subject matter which is paraphrased below.

The Book of Invasions is a twelfth-century chronicle of the various pre-Christian colonisations of Ireland. The race who occupied the country before the Gaelic people were the Tuatha De Danaan (The peoples of the goddess Danaan). While their origins are unclear, the Tuatha were a mystical race, handsome and learned, elegantly dressed, expert in every art and science, and supreme masters of wizardry. A brave race, the leaders of the Tuatha were first and foremost wizards, and warriors second, whose victories were gained more by superior knowledge and magic than combat.

The Tuatha De Danaan occupied Ireland in relative peace until the arrival of the Milesian warriors. After a defeat at the battle of Tailcann, the Tuatha vanished from the country. Tradition and popular belief hold that the Tuatha transformed themselves into the Sluagh Sidhe (The Fairy Host) and, taking their secrets and arts with them, entered an occult realm where they remain to this day.

In pre-Christian Ireland, there were three principal categories of song called Geantrai (the joyous strain), Goltrai (the lamenting strain) and Suantrai (the sleep strain.) *The Book of Invasions (A Celtic Symphony)* is divided into three movements. The first, subtitled 'Geantrai – When Gods Walked the Earth', takes up all of the first side of vinyl. The second and third movements ('Goltrai – The Pursuit of Diarmaid and Grainne'; and 'Suantrai – The Living End') occupies side two.

'First Movement; Geantrai'
'When Gods Walked the Earth'

A quotation from *The Book of Invasions* chronicle sets the scene;

> In this way, they came, in dark clouds over the air, by might of druidry, and they landed on a mountain in Connaught. Thereafter the Tuatha De Danaan brought a darkness over the sun and the moon, for a space of three days and three nights. They demanded battle or kingship of the Fir Bolg.

The Fir Bolg was a race similar to the Picts, who were then defeated by the Tuatha at the Plain of the Pillars in Moytura, County Sligo. It wasn't until after the Second Battle of Moytura, and a victory over the loathsome Fomhoire, ancient enemies of cosmic order, that the Tuatha were able to live in peace.

'Daybreak' (2.30)

This overture is a cleverly written, tightly arranged instrumental which shines light on some, but not all, of the musical themes which are to follow in the first movement. The central melody is taken from a traditional Irish drinking song which translates as 'It is day'. The three-note fanfare phrase is based on a G major triad and, according to Lockhart:

> ...the idea was to have this very basic sound rising out of the mist and those first three notes of 'Daybreak' correspond exactly with the opening notes of the traditional tune. The guy playing those notes on a trumpet was Ray Moore, a session player that Alan hired...

In case any fans were concerned about the use of a brass instrument to open the album, such fears were soon allayed. The trumpet motif is joined by a steady, quaver-based drone on the electric mandolin, with electric guitar taking over the melody ten seconds in and showcasing some clever open-string harmonics. Behind this is an impressive mix of cymbal swells and choral-style backing vocals.

45 seconds in and this section (minus the trumpet introduction) is repeated with the mandolin playing a counterpoint melody based around arpeggios, whilst bass, drums, and some 'way-back-in-the-mix' keyboards provide a solid bedrock of rhythm and harmony. This texture is maintained for a repeat of this section of music, with Fean giving a nod to Thin Lizzy in his use of overdriven, harmonised guitars playing the melody.

At 1.44, a new mood is briefly featured just using flute, whistle and keyboards. Lockhart related:

> (The melody here) is taken from a Galway lament called 'Anach Cuan' written about some villagers who set off from the shores of Lough Corrib and were drowned when their boat sank.

At 2.00, the mood changes abruptly again; the opening phrase appears on the organ and moves into the parallel key of G minor. Overdriven guitar, bass and drums provide an answering heavy power-chord phrase based around a C major triad. The organ drops down a tone into the F minor triad, with the response from the rhythm section being a Bb major triad. A further shift down a semitone to an E minor triad is followed with a reply triad in A major, before the track concludes on a final E minor triad from all players. 'Daybreak' is impressive, anthemic, and highly indicative of what is to come.

'March From Trouble' (0.51)

Giving a nice touch of continuity, this short instrumental, an adaptation of the traditional tune 'Brian Boru's March', is also in E minor. The first theme is played on keyboards, with acoustic guitar providing the accompaniment. The second part of the tune moves into G major, with flute being added to the texture. This comes to a sudden stop at the end of the appropriate phrase as the first classic of the album begins...

'Trouble (With a Capital T)' (3.23)

A breathy 'rock' flute and overdriven guitar takes the second melody from 'Brian Boru's March' and moves it from its previous lilting 6/8 time into a straight, 'four-to-the floor' driving rhythm. Bass, drums, keyboards (a Hohner Clavinet), and mandolin drive the music along at a brisk tempo.

The first vocal appearance is Fean's; 'High on the mountain stands a boat…' with O'Connor joining for the second half of the verse: 'Night after night I don't believe…'. The chorus is fantastic, with the flute adding the amended 'Brian Boru March' melody in for good measure. After a second verse and chorus, there is an excellent instrumental section (1.47 – 2.08) where harmonised guitars and flutes weave fresh melodies in counterpoint, coming to a sudden three-crotchet beat long rest.

The introduction is heard again, and in a live situation, this is a spine-tingling moment. It's the perfect time for enthusiastic appreciation and the audience always delivered. Then, and this is purely a personal bug-bear, the second half of the third verse is a repeat of the first half of the first. Such a device always strikes me as lazy writing, and given Carr's skills as a lyricist, and the album's broad subject matter, new words should be appearing here. The chorus is repeated and the introduction reprised for a final time with the entire band playing with intensity, the song coming to a sharp end in time for the next track, which, almost unbelievably, is even better.

My only criticism, more of a missed opportunity really, is that, given the flow of one track into another throughout the movement, there was the possibility for the first beat of the introduction to 'The Power and the Glory' to be placed on the final beat of 'Trouble (With a Capital T)' to provide an effective merge between the two songs. The gap may have been created as the songs are in different keys (E minor and F sharp minor, respectively), but such a device would have added even greater cohesion to the first movement.

'The Power and the Glory' (3.57)

This song, backed with 'Sir Festus Burke', was released as a single in the UK on 25 July 1977. Opening with a rousing and heroic sounding church organ theme, 'The Power and the Glory' soon turns into an addictive chugging rocker with some excellent lyrics: 'Into the flash of the lightning star-riders are hurled, see them bumping and grinding, bareback on the wheels of the world'. An overdriven electric guitar provides a neat melodic counterpoint to the vocal phrases, and organ joins the texture again for the second half of the verse.

The chorus, with its sing-a-long refrain, benefits from some beefed-up guitar and some neat bluesy overlaid phrases, before the introduction is reprised with guitar, bass, and drums grooving away effortlessly. The second verse contains the memorable lines 'People say we've got the power, the phrase I think is hearts and minds', and 'Not so much teachers as fighters, and what we teach is how to fight.'

A second chorus leads the song out of rock land into more familiar Horslips territory, with a highly effective, busy, and very melodic violin solo over the verse chord sequence and texture. A third chorus is extended by an extra two refrains, with the final words ('We're gonna take it, we're gonna take it') repeated. The underlying power chord progression segues smoothly into ...

'The Rocks Remain' (2.49)
...a lightening of mood with arpeggiated electric and acoustic guitars, keyboards, hi-hat and tambourine, and a tuneful bass line providing a relaxed feel to the sole ballad of the first movement. Written primarily by Devlin, there is a hint of mid-period Beatles to the composition. Originally titled 'Mother of Pearl', Carr's talent as a wordsmith is again on display: 'Precious stones and stolen thrones vanish in a day. Your golden rings, your silver rings will crumble and decay'. The melody for these lines is sung by two voices, with Devlin's singular vocal taking care of the rest of the verse: 'Silks and satins and crimson velvet will someday fade away.' The unison singing returns for the final lines: 'But the stones will stand across the land, and love will have it's day.'

The second verse has a philosophical air to it; 'Change will come to everyone, never question why', with the flute adding brief phrases in between the lines. A bridge section (1.20 – 1.37) features more harmonised singing ('I can see the lights below us, twinkle like the stars, and I know they're waiting patiently for the day to break again.') This leads into a slide guitar solo for the first eight bars with a counterpoint flute melody, a four-bar section of just a climbing guitar line, before four more bars of slide and flute.

The third verse continues the lyrical eloquence: 'Distant skies, different eyes, change has come to fast, and a mother of pearl, distant girl, clutches at the past.' The closing stanza emphasises the track's theme of longevity: 'But in the sunset, I see your eyes and they tell me nothing's lost'. The final words ('strong love') carries over the 'three repetitions' trick of the coda of 'The Power and the Glory', ending the song on a satisfying D major chord.

'Dusk' (0.38)
This short instrumental is a reprise of the heavier section of 'Daybreak' (2.00 onwards), with the 'response' triads being replaced by the violin playing 'Toss the Feathers' backed by a solid bodhran beat. Here the music acts as a prelude for the song it is about to segue into. The fourth part of the sequence is cut short with the emergence of (sorry, 'Dearg Doom' fans) Fean's finest contribution to the Horslips canon...

'Sword of Light' (4.57)
Written by Lockhart and Carr, and sung by Fean, the guitarist's reinterpretation of 'Toss the Feathers' is the central theme of this, the band's finest four minutes and 57 seconds. Mirrored by the keyboards and interspersed with bass and drum power chord smashes, the introduction shows just what the listener has in store.

A new, nifty guitar riff replaces 'Toss the Feathers' as the track settles into a fabulous groove, driven along by energetic drumming. 'Toss the Feathers' reappears just prior to Fean's excellent vocal. For the pre-chorus, concertina joins the mix: 'Walking hand in hand with silver, close as gold to kiss. Only lovers left alive and they're swallowed in the mist'. The chorus to 'Sword of Light' is the song, and possibly the album's vocal highlight. Harmonised vocals and an overwhelming sense of spirit dominate here, with a brief instrumental interlude acting as a link to the second verse and chorus.

At 2.49, an instrumental section featuring the 'nifty riff' again (this time in just the right stereo channel, and a delayed guitar in the left channel) appears, with the phrase being repeated four times without any rhythmic backing. Keyboards are added for the third and fourth repeats, and bass and drums join in for the final four play-throughs as the music builds into the third verse, which, disappointingly, is a re-run of the first verse, and a final chorus.

If the chorus is the vocal peak of *The Book of Invasions*, the song's coda section (4.07 – 4.57) is its instrumental pinnacle. The 'Toss the Feathers' riff is reprised in the right stereo channel, whilst in the left channel, the guitar strings are muted and vigorously strummed, giving a percussive effect against the main riff. Keyboards join in and the bass and drum power chord smashes return in an unexpected fashion; two, then one, then another, finally two more, and the rhythm section kicks back in, driving the track along to its end. The 'delay' guitar riff is reprised over a heavy bass drum beat, and a quick three-note rising phrase finishes off the song, moving it quickly into...

'Dark' (1.38)

...the 'It is Day' theme reappears, played with guitar harmonics, before an arpeggiated sequence drops us back into the familiar melody with harmonised guitars, keyboards, electric mandolin, bass and drums all featuring in an excellently arranged and well-balanced mix.

47 seconds in, the 'Anach Cuan' melody and instrumentation returns, and at 1.02, the trumpet fanfare, which began the movement, is heard again. Power chords darken the mood with the pattern following the same harmonic descent which featured in 'Daybreak', the track finishing on a single sustained keyboard chord.

'Second Movement; Goltrai'
'The Pursuit of Diarmaid and Grainne'

Grainne, a pretty young girl, is forced to marry the elderly Fionn MacCumhaill. At the wedding feast, she drugs all the guests except Fionn's friend, Diarmaid, a warrior and ladies' man, whom she places under 'geassa' (a sacred magic obligation) to elope with her. Though he is reluctant to betray his friend, Diarmaid is compelled to obey. Their wanderings are filled with fantastic adventures and eventually, they become lovers. It takes the god Oenghus to make peace between the rivals and Diarmaid and Grainne live happily for years until one day, while hunting a magic boar with Fionn, Diarmaid is mortally wounded. Only Fionn has the power to save him, but he prefers to take revenge and so Diarmaid dies. The trio seem to have supernatural origins and it would appear we are witnessing the rivalry between a younger and an older deity for the possession of a goddess.

'Warm Sweet Breath of Love' (3.26)
The main melodic theme of the second movement is the traditional tune 'My Lagan Love', a beautiful slow air, played as an introduction here on concertina.

Devlin notes that the song had influences:

> With 'Warm Sweet Breath of Love', I was trying to write a stylistic response to Thin Lizzy's 'Running Back' from *Jailbreak* (1976), but the Beatle influences really poke through as well, and so it's an interesting blend that shows us at our most commercial.

There are certainly similarities between the two songs; both have a 'shuffle' rhythm and are set in 12/8 time, both are in major keys (A for Lizzy, C for Horslips), and the reliance on a I, IV, V chord sequence pervades both tracks. However, whereas Lizzy kept to their usual rock instrumentation for their song (plus a charming electric piano melody line), Horslips throw in a barrage of traditional instruments into this highly catchy song. Piano, concertina, and mandolin feature heavily, along with some harmonised electric guitars *a la* Lizzy.

Devlin's vocals suit this relaxed and yet still rocking song, and there are some more evocative lyrics: 'They've pursued us now it seems forever, they've caught up with us like time. They've followed us close down every misbegotten highway they haunt us like our crime.' The only disappointment in this otherwise first-class number is the repeated use of the first verse for the post-instrumental third verse. In all other regards, this is a further example of high-class songwriting, arrangement, and performance which, surprisingly, comes to a definitive end rather than fading away on its rolling rhythm.

'Warm Sweet Breath of Love' (backed with 'King of Morning, Queen of Day') was released as a single in the UK on 25 February 1977. It was 'picked up' by the legendary Irish broadcaster Terry Wogan, who played it on his Radio 2 show. This exposure enhanced sales to an unprecedented degree.

'Fantasia (My Lagan Love)' (2.55)
Commenting on the use of 'My Lagan Love' Fean said:

> Jim played 'My Lagan Love' to us on flute while we were writing the album. The idea was to use it as a repetitive theme to link some of the songs, but also to feature it as a main track, speeding up the tempo of what was usually

performed as a slow air by so many artists. Like 'King of the Fairies', it was a very well-known Irish song, and our challenge was to bring it into the modern rock context.

The outstanding feature of this expansive instrumental is the sound of Fean's Gibson Les Paul Goldtop guitar. From the 'violined' opening phrases, to his full-blooded melodic tone throughout the rest of the track, the guitarist is the centrepiece of this very fine reinvention of a very old tune, first collected in 1903 in County Donegal.

After the atmospheric introduction, the track sets forth at a brisk tempo with the guitar being backed initially by just bass and drums. A strummed steel strung guitar is added at 0.37, with keyboards joining at 1.09. At 1.21, the drum rhythm becomes more relaxed as a second guitar is heard, providing a contrasting, bluesy melody to the rich, creamy guitar sound of the main tune.

At 1.52, the rhythmic drive returns and some energetic violin playing is added. At 2.23, the bluesy counterpoint section, with added flute, reappears briefly before 'Fantasia' steams to a sudden, tight end. This is a wonderful instrumental with the skilful arrangement showing the many-faceted skills of the band in the best light.

'King of Morning, Queen of Day' (4.32)

Originally titled 'Kings and Queens' (the name was changed at the artwork stage of the album), the chorus of the final song of the second movement is based on the 'Kilfenora Jig', originally found in County Clare.

Beginning with a reprise of the introduction to 'Fantasia', a Fender Rhodes electric piano starts the song off proper together with some tasteful guitar arpeggios, creating a pleasing, pastoral feel. Prominent bass is added, and the verse lyrics are sung in harmony – a neat touch. A triplet-based, military-style drum rhythm appears, with further guitar contributions as the volume increases, building dramatically into the pre-chorus lines: 'So don't you cry, don't you fear, wipe away each lonely tear'.

The chorus itself is magnificent; its lyrics are 'unashamedly borrowed' (according to Lockhart) from 'A Match', a poem by the splendidly named English poet, Algernon Charles Swinburne (1837 – 1909) whose original lines read:

If you were queen of pleasure, and I were king of pain.
We'd hunt down love together, pluck out his flying feather,
And teach his feet a measure, and find his mouth a rein.
If you were queen of pleasure, and I were king of pain.

In Carr's hands, this becomes: 'If I were king of morning, and you were queen of day, we'd love all summer long, together love would find a way. If I were king of evening and you were queen of night, we'd pass the time in pleasure, we'd love until the morning light. If I were king of pleasure and you were queen of pain, you would love me.'

Behind this is a fantastic keyboard, bass and drum backing, syncopating the last line as the music calms for the second verse, which adds the driving rhythm section and plenty of overdriven guitar. A second chorus leads into a guitar solo (3.03 – 3.24) over the verse chord progression.

And then they go and let themselves down again. The third verse is a re-run of the first, again. Amongst all the excellent playing, melodies, and *brio* of the song, this is small critical beer, but a different third verse would have fleshed out the characters and story of Diarmaid and Grainne further. A final chorus rounds off this fantastic track, and the movement on a single sustained G major chord ties this song neatly into ...

'Third Movement; Suantrai'
'The Living End'

The Tuatha's reign ended when they were defeated by the Sons of Mil at Tailteann, County Meath. The newcomers then divided Ireland in two. The half that was underground became the Tuatha's, and the other half was given to the Sons of Mil. It has been argued that the Battle of Tailteann could have been a bloodless affair because Tailteann was the site of the Tuatha's games, and because the Milesians are known to have been in awe of the Tuatha's druidic powers. Their first confrontation was alarming for the Milesians, who faced spectres and monsters conjured by the Tuatha. Honourable in defeat, the Tuatha retired to a hidden world parallel to ours where life, immortal, goes on as before.

'Sideways to the Sun' (4.46)

Also in G major, which gives a stylish continuity between the second and third movements, 'Sideways to the Sun' opens with 'Slan Cois Maigh', a slow air from County Mayo. Violin and electric guitar play this hauntingly beautiful tune in harmony, with subtle, sustained keyboards in the background and bass and drums joining in at 1.41. Carr explained his choice of words:

> In the two verses, as in the title, the 'voice' is of the race we only know from lore and legend, and through intuition. It's that of the inhabitants of another spiritual plane, a place where the normal laws of physics don't apply.

The music gradually develops into the song itself with more excellent lyrics, especially with the second verse: 'We're the mystery of the lake when the waters still. We're the laughter in the twilight you can hear behind the hill....'. The tempo is steady, the instrument's melodies weave in and out of each other, and the vocals are again sung in harmony. This is highly impressive stuff; a ballad with as much care and attention to detail paid in all departments as to the album's rockier tracks.

An instrumental section (3.01 – 3.42) reprises 'Slan Cois Maigh' with bass and drums continuing their relentless pulse behind the enchanting melodies. The music melds the traditional air with the song's chorus chord progression to bring in the final verse. Argh! It happens again – verse three is a repeated verse two. At the risk of sounding like a broken record, a smudged CD, or an interrupted download, surely more words could have been written to continue the theme of this otherwise fantastic song.

Five 'Sideways to the Sun' repeats and a swirling keyboard solo bring the song to a close with a clever key change; the chords move from repeated G major and C major to D minor, which acts as a segue into...

'Drive the Cold Winter Away' (0.35)

...this very short instrumental is, of course, familiar having been the title track of the previous album. Here acoustic guitar and concertina play the music which shifts quickly into the introduction of ...

'Ride to Hell' (4.10)

...where the flute introduces a new melody over the guitar and concertina, as the underlying chord sequence (which will form the basis of the verse) twists and turns its way into the vocals of the final track.

Carr again provided an explanation of the lyrics:

> 'Ride to Hell' is a fairytale that was written to provide the album with an epilogue. As I speculated on the Tuatha's decision to go underground or into a parallel universe or psychic realm, I automatically came to consider the many old folk tales that tell of strange occurrences and happenings at the fairy rath, usually after dark. Every tribe, society and nation has its own fairy tales. There are plenty of stories of people being tempted to enter the fairy realm. Some came back. Others were lost forever. I wondered what it might be like to be propositioned in such a way. And who, or what, might offer such enticement? Usually, it was the promise of a pot of gold, vast treasures or eternal youth that swayed the individual.

'Ride to Hell' is an excellent, rocking conclusion to the album. The first verse follows the relaxed, pastoral feel of the introduction with acoustic guitar, concertina, and flute playing off each other until, 42 seconds in, a rising organ ostinato paves the way for a return to heaviness, with a strident cowbell much to the fore. A grinding combination of overdriven guitar, organ, bass and drums back the hard-edged lyrics sung by Devlin: 'You'll find him hard to recognise cos he won't dress in black. He wears a suit of gold lame with velvet front and back. But he can touch your trembling heart, can touch your very soul. He'll take you with him when he leaves, he'll make your dreams turn old'.

Whilst the lyrics are a direct repeat of the acoustic section of the song, the change of instrumentation and tempo means that, this time, the repetition does not grate. The words acquire fresh impetus resulting from the change of texture.

The second verse is just as strong and builds into a crescendo for the chorus. This is superb, with powerful drumming and harmonised vocals, plus plenty of atmospheric reverb. This leads into an instrumental section (1.52 – 2.13) which is reminiscent of Emerson, Lake and Palmer; here, Lockhart gives the song a 'prog rock meets Baroque' style keyboard solo. Instrumental duties are then passed over to a soaring violin solo (2.14 – 2.33). The third verse continues against the rock backdrop, with another fantastic build into the final chorus, with the song coming to what sounds like an end at 3.20.

However, there's a further verse (see, you can write them!) which is set against the initial acoustic backing: 'He's sure to come-a-calling when the shades of night are drawn. A twisted blackthorn in his hand, he'll linger until dawn. You wish to stay forever young, but only he knows how. It's his blessing, it's his curse, and it's your decision now…'. The song concludes with a gentle mix of acoustic guitar open string 'natural' harmonics, flute, and concertina, the music fading to nothing, creating a sense of ambivalence. What would you do in the circumstances?

Emphasising the creative high watermark which *The Book of Invasions* represented, there was a song left over. Lockhart recounts:

> The album was so well planned out that only one number was missing from the line-up we sketched out. 'The Rights of Man', a traditional Irish hornpipe, was destined to be on the album and we'd been playing it live, but as the sessions developed, it didn't sit well with the rest of the tracks, so we never got to record it.

A live recording of this instrumental is featured on Disc 16: Live In Berlin 1976 on *More Than You Can Chew*.

Tracks From the Vaults (1977)

Personnel:
Eamon Carr: drums, bodrahn, percussion
Barry Devlin: bass, vocals
John Fean: guitar, banjo, vocals
Jim Lockhart: keyboards, flute, tin whistle, vocals
Charles O'Connor: fiddle, mandolin, concertina, vocals
Declan Sinnott: Guitar on 'Motorway Madness', 'Johnny's Wedding' and 'Flower Amang Them All'
Gus Guest: Guitar on 'Green Gravel', and 'The Fairy King'
Producers: Various, as noted
Recorded at various locations, as noted
All tracks composed/arranged by Carr, Devlin, Fean, O'Connor, and Lockhart
Released on 7 May 1977
Issued on Oats Records in Ireland (M0013)

1977 saw the finalisation of a new international record deal for the band, with Michael Deeny returning to ensure successful negotiations with DJM Records. Regular touring continued of both Ireland and the United Kingdom, and in the meantime, fans were treated to this 'stop-gap' compilation of rare tracks, designed to build on the success of *The Book of Invasions.*

The cover, a pastiche of a Marvel-style comic, looked tacky and cheap. O'Connor elucidated:

> There was little continuity between album designs, and the cover of *Tracks From the Vaults* serves as evidence, but does it matter? Eamon liked that Marvel comic idea, as one might expect, and I drew the basis of it one night after coming home from a gig slightly worse for alcohol. This was normal for me if I couldn't sleep. I gave myself the design credit under the name 'Les Lee Superior' and John Webb produced the final print-ready artwork. We could have achieved a better result if we'd given the job to a genuine comic artist. Someone from 2000AD would have been ideal as would Toko Mata style, but we didn't have a superstar art budget.

The design, featuring a pair of long-nailed, bony green hands over a black and pink background, referenced some of the album's songs in amusing fashion: 'Dare you revisit 'The Green Gravel?', 'Solved! The Lipstick Mystery', 'Secret Origins of 'Dearg Doom'', and so on. The monster from *The Unfortunate Cup of Tea!* also makes a cameo appearance in cartoon form with a word bubble saying 'Too good to waste'.

'Motorway Madness' (3.14)

Not previously on an album, this song featured in the band's early live sets and was recorded at Trend Studios by Fred Meijer in October 1971.

'Motorway Madness' is a guitar, bass, and drum-heavy, taut little rocker, with a catchy chorus. There is, however, no trace of any traditional instrumentation to separate this song from a host of like-minded pop-rock band singles of the time. Lyrically, it manages to mix the banal ('You handled the car like you handled a gun, as we headed towards the city we were on the run') with indications of greater talent ('Deaf to the sirens growing near, insensitive to promises, hopes, and fears'.)

The song chugs along at a middling tempo for its duration, with Devlin's vocals sounding strained at times. The organ contributions in the pre-chorus are too high in the mix, which overall sounds muddled and muddy. The chorus itself is twee and irritatingly catchy in equal measure. Sinnott weaves his bluesy, distorted electric guitar lines with flair and dexterity throughout.

'Motorway Madness' is, of course, of great interest to fans as a slice of the band's musical history, but it's nobody's lost classic by any means. It is also, rather worryingly, similar to the template for the material served up on the epic disappointment that would be *Short Stories, Tall Tales* nearly a decade later.

'Johnny's Wedding' (3.23)

Recorded at Trend Studios in January 1972 at the same time as 'Flower Amang Them All' and 'Knocken Free', and released on 17 March, 'Johnny's Wedding' was again produced by Fred Meijer. It was the band's first hit single release, being restricted solely to Ireland alone, where it spent three weeks in the charts, peaking at number ten.

This is much more like it. 'Johnny's Wedding' is a fast-paced instrumental which mixes some manic musicianship with an interesting arrangement, spoilt only by the heavy-on-the-reverb production. This traditional tune gets the full Horslips treatment, opening with some harmonised electric guitars over a powerful rhythm section which builds in intensity. O'Connor takes over the melody on his electric mandolin 28 seconds in. Here the degree of reverb added to the melody heightens, rather than obscures, his playing.

At 1.46, Sinnott bursts in with two intertwining distorted solos bouncing off each other over some thunderous drumming. At 2.12, there is a change of mood; a vigorously strummed acoustic guitar is now heard, with Lockhart adding a flute solo. The bass and drums grow again, with more fretboard flurries, before the track comes to a syncopated end at 3.04.

Described in the sleeve notes as 'Jim's little joke', Lockhart then plays a simple arrangement of the opening bars of the Mendelsohn's 'Wedding March' on the piano.

'Flower Amang Them All' (2.32)

The B side to the 'Johnny's Wedding' single, 'Flower Amang Them All', is a gently lilting instrumental featuring just concertina, tin whistle, acoustic guitar, bass, and bongos. It would later go on to become the theme for *RTÉ Radio's* popular '301' show, and, of course, was rerecorded for *Happy to Meet...*

After the frantic energy of 'Johnny's Wedding', 'Flower Amang Them All' shows a softer side to the band without any rock drums or distorted guitar. It would have been easy to 'heavy' this track up, but the band clearly wanted to show their audience that there was much more to them than just giving traditional tunes a damned good thrashing.

'Green Gravel' (3.24)

The band's second single, and the only one to showcase short-lived guitarist Gus Guest, was recorded at Trend Studios in June 1972, again with Fred Meijer acting as engineer. Released on 25 August, the single hit the top 20 in its first week of release.

A faded-in introduction of strummed acoustic guitar and mandolin is soon overlaid with a beautifully distorted electric guitar melody, to which bass and drums are quickly added. 30 seconds in and a secondary melody appears with concertina and keyboards being added to the mix. Devlin's vocals have too much reverb applied to them and are too far back in the mix, the instruments tending to stiffle his performance.

The album sleeve notes that 'this Ulster version is a children's skipping song, but the song is really a sad one. 'Green Gravel' is a corruption of 'Green Grave' and the song is about the death of a young and beautiful girl. We've used the middle eight from a related song, 'Young girl cut down in her prime', versions of which include 'St. James Infirmary' and 'The Unfortunate Rake''.

At 1.28, the light-hearted musical feel and 3/4 time signature is dispensed with, and a very doomy combination of distorted guitar and a heavy bass drum set the music in 2/4 time. O'Connor's vocals are heartfelt and treated with plenty of reverb to produce a genuinely dark atmosphere. The original texture and time signature is restored at 1.56, with the organ adding much to the manic energy of the short instrumental section. The lyrics are repeated with several voices singing in harmony. 'Green Gravel' concludes with a gritty electric guitar solo as the backing instrumentation disappears, leaving just Guest, Devlin, and Carr playing into the final fade.

'The Fairy King' (3.57)

The B-side to 'Green Gravel' is a stunningly beautiful instrumental. 'The Fairy King' is described in the sleeve notes as an ancient harp tune which is coupled with the Welsh 'Blodau'r Drain' ('Flowers of the Thorn')

Opening with a Renaissance-sounding duet between mandolin and acoustic guitar, it is atmospheric, melodic, and proof of the power of allowing space around music. No other instruments play in this first section, the mandolin and guitar are enough.

After a brief fingerpicked acoustic guitar reprise of the melody (1.53 – 2.08), O'Connor takes over the melody on concertina, with flute providing soft support in the background. There is some gentle bodhran playing as a light rhythmic backdrop to the interweaving melodies. At 3.01, the flute takes centre stage, with the concertina playing a harmony line from 3.13 as the graceful guitar arpeggios continue. The track enters its coda section, with the percussion becoming more prominent as the music slows to a sad end.

'Dearg Doom' (3.18)

This is an alternate mix (described in the sleeve notes as 'definitive') of the classic song released as a single just in Germany in 1974, where it became a hit. This version produced by Fryer at the Manor Studios' is fundamentally the same as the track on *Danceball Sweethearts* with a few noticeable differences.

The cymbal introduction is slightly longer, the vocals, guitar and drums are treated with a much higher degree of reverb, and the bass line is 'dry' and consequently sounds further forward in the mix. Whilst it's interesting to hear a different interpretation of the song from a producer's ear-point, the album original is better than this. Or perhaps that's just over-familiarity talking ...

'The High Reel' (2.42)

Recorded at the Manor Studios with Alan O'Duffy in April 1973 and mixed at Olympic Studios, the track would later be included on later pressings of the band's debut album when it appeared on the Atco label. It was also the B-side of the Irish single release of 'Dearg Doom', as well as the first British single on RCA Records, 'Furniture'.

'The High Reel' is a glorious riot of a track. The double-tracked violin melody is punctuated with heavy power chords and a frantic rhythm section is unleashed, turning the familiar folk tune into a hard rock ceilidh. At 1.05, the music starts to sound more traditional as the violin melody is joined by banjo, with handclap accompaniment in the background on the second and fourth beats of each bar. A syncopated bass and jazz-like electric guitar progression add to the fun. This continues at 1.52 with the melody instruments dropping out and a brief duet between rhythm guitar and keyboards changes the feel for eight bars, whilst the track is held together by some enthusiastic tambourine work.

At 2.07, having had a much-needed minutes rest, the violin explodes back into the mix with a variation of the opening tune, backed with more aggressive power chords. The rhythm kicks in, driving the tune towards a busy end. The stark increase in tempo towards the finish of the track is a clear indication of just how much fun the band had when recording this. The musicianship, spirit, and clever arrangement mark this track as a hidden gem in the Horslips back catalogue.

'King of the Fairies' (3.19)

Recorded at Rockfield Studios in June 1974 and produced by Fryer, 'King of the Fairies' was released as a single in Ireland on 8 July 1974. This classic track spent five weeks on the chart, peaking at number seven.

The differences between this and the version on *Danceball Sweethearts*, such as they are, are negligible and relate entirely to the recording levels of the interweaving individual instruments

'Phil the Fluter's Rag' (2.32)
The B-side of the 'King of the Fairies' single is a charming up-tempo duet between rhythmic acoustic guitar in the left stereo channel, and high-speed mandolin melody in the right. At 1.17, with a blast of inspirational energy, the two swap roles as Fean plays a very fine country-style flat-pick solo against O'Connor's staccato chord stabs on the second and fourth beats of each bar. At 1.33, the original tune and arrangement returns and, at 1.51, the tempo gets even faster for a highly dexterous coda section. 'Phil the Fluter's Rag' concludes with a reprise of the highly melodic introduction, ending on an off-beat guitar chord stab.

'Come Back Beatles' (3.25)
Horslips were huge fans of The Beatles and, during the sessions that led to *The Unfortunate Cup of Tea!*, they recorded this tribute single. Realising the song couldn't go out under the Horslips name, a band title was invented ('Lipstick') and various record companies were approached. The prevailing view at the time was that The Beatles were out of fashion and that newer pop bands (The Bay City Rollers, for example) were in vogue instead.

Then EMI rereleased all the original Beatles singles and most of them entered the charts – again! Suddenly the strange Irish group with their tribute song struck a chord in the record companies' memory banks and, according to Carr: '...offers poured in. Being stubborn, we delighted in telling them we had moved on.'

One of the few companies Horslips hadn't approached was Polydor who agreed to release the single. At the time, the only real way to achieve any likelihood of commercial success was to be placed on a playlist at the BBC. This didn't happen, but as Carr puts it, 'it was fun while it lasted'.

The single 'Come Back Beatles' backed with 'The Fab Four-Four' was released on 23 April 1976. 'Come Back Beatles' is no pastiche, but it certainly takes several elements of The Beatles' music and mixes them together in a catchy and happily tuneful way. Opening with some enthusiastic crowd noise, the song is based around a 'Ticket to Ride' style ostinato, but at a quicker tempo. The vocals are harmonised, there's plenty of percussion and the chorus is highly reminiscent of the band's early 1960s-era output. At 1.14, the guitar riff from 'Day Tripper' makes a brief appearance with Devlin's McCartney-esque bass scoops blending with the reappearing crowd noise.

A second verse lyrically references The Cavern, and the songs 'Rain' and 'Here Comes the Sun'. A two-bar extract of 'I Want to Hold Your Hand' also makes a very brief appearance. Another chorus is followed by a short excerpt from the guitar part for 'Ticket to Ride', and then a further chorus. After this, it's time for a quick version of the magnificent 'Paperback Writer' guitar riff at 2.43. A further chorus amid more crowd noise brings the track to a 'live' end'.

'The Fab Four-Four' (2.47)
The album sleeve notes state:

> This began life as a backing track for a song called 'I'm in a Hole'. A rethink and a tip-of-the-hat to Booker T and The MG's gave a flip side to 'Come Back Beatles'.

Similarly recorded at Rockfield Studios under the guiding hands of Fryer, this instrumental is dominated by lightly distorted guitar solos and decorative organ fills. Although brisk of tempo and well played it is, like all instrumentals without a truly strong central melody, a bit dull after a while. The ending is unexpected, coming as it does on a repeated syncopated bass note.

'Daybreak' (3.22)
Now, this *is* interesting. 'Daybreak' (the single) is different to 'Daybreak' (the album track). Recorded with engineer Pat Morley at Dublin Sound Studios and released as a single in July 1976, this version spent 22 weeks on the Irish charts.

As well as being almost a minute longer, the overall sound lacks some of the polish of O'Duffy's production skills. The harmonised guitars are absent prior to the 'Anach Cuan' section; Fean merely plays the initial single-line melody as before.

The most significant changes comes after the 'Anach Cuan' music. The mood change into G minor (with its corresponding doom-laden fanfare response from guitar, bass and drums) is missing; instead, the original guitar melody is repeated briefly, this time with the harmony guitar lines back in their familiar place. At 2.17, the trumpet fanfare is reprised (in the major key) with matching major triad power chords. This section is transposed up a tone to A major and continues to a fade.

Perhaps it was felt that maintaining the positive melodic framework worked better for a single rather than the more portentous music which followed the 'Anach Cuan' section on the album version. Whatever the actual intention, this 'Daybreak' is a fascinating insight into the creative process at work; neither version is *better* than the other, but the more familiar album track is superior both in composition and arrangement.

'Oisin's Tune' (2.30)
According to the album sleeve notes, this 'first came to light on poet Paul Muldoon's St. Patrick's Day radio play in 1976.' The track was rearranged and recorded at Avondale Studios with Pat Gibbons behind the desk. It became the B-side to the 'Daybreak' single.

The track is an instrumental in two distinct parts; the first begins with a pulsing, drone-like ostinato on acoustic guitar and mandolin, over which the 'Daybreak' melody is played four times in its post-'Anach Cuan' minor key setting on the concertina. The coda to this section has the 'response' melody played three times, leading neatly into Carr's highly rhythmic bodhran playing 52 seconds in.

'Oisin's Tune' itself then takes flight at a faster tempo and with a brighter sound and feel to it. Bodrahn, acoustic guitar and concertina all sound in fine form. At 1.29, a harmonising concertina melody is added, which continues for the rest of this very enjoyable, traditional-sounding track.

Aliens (1977)

Personnel:
Eamon Carr: drums, percussion
Barry Devlin: bass, vocals
John Fean: guitar, vocals
Jim Lockhart: keyboards, flute
Charles O'Connor: fiddle, mandolin, vocals
Recorded at Lombard Sound Studios, Dublin
Produced by Alan O'Duffy and Horslips
Engineered by Alan O'Duffy
All tracks composed/arranged by Carr, Devlin, Fean, O'Connor, and Lockhart
Released on 4 November 1977
Issued on Oats Records in Ireland (M0014), RCA in the UK (DJF 20519), and DJM DJLPA- 16 (USA)

In the UK, 1977 saw the emergence of punk as a musical force to be reckoned with. Meanwhile, in America, 'AOR' (Adult Orientated Rock) dominated the airwaves; Boston, Fleetwood Mac, *et al* were massive acts, both in terms of record sales and concert attendance. Into this mix, Horslips now threw their collective hats with some good-to-mixed results.

Cinemas were filled with audiences entranced by the likes of *Close Encounters of the Third Kind* and *Star Wars*. Any fans who thought the band was cashing in on these newly popular phenomena with their new album were mistaken. The inner sleeve of *Aliens* contained the following:

> As chronicled in *The Book of Invasions*, the Sons of Mil inherited Ireland from the mystical Tuatha De Danaan in 350 BC. The 1840s were the Famine Years and once again the Sons Of Mil were driven to search for a new home. Exiled, they were fated to begin a new life as aliens.

Aliens was recorded in the autumn of 1977 following tours of Ireland, the United Kingdom, and Europe. With the album finished, the band undertook their first full-scale tour of America, which included playing as support to arena acts, including Blue Öyster Cult, Molly Hatchet, and Black Oak Arkansas. Songs from the new album were given prominence. As Devlin said:

> We were forever reaching into ourselves to establish roots that we could relate to. Through the tours that promoted *The Book of Invasions* in the States, we were living the American experience. At that point, I think we all agreed that we'd done as much as we could with ancient mythology and decided to tell a comparatively modern tale that had parallels with our own situation new to this huge continent. *Aliens* was reaching out beyond our cultural roots.

Aliens is the second in the trilogy of albums dealing with the themes of exile and immigration. With this release, the band focused on the sufferers of the Irish Potato Famine who had migrated to America in the 1840s. Not a very 'rock'n'roll' subject matter, you might think, and this was also the reaction from their record company in America. However, Horslips, with their gift for dealing with serious ideas within the context of excellent songs delivered the goods again. The melodies are strong and the lyrics are thoughtful, intelligent, and provoking. The dialling down of the traditional instrumentation and the streamlining of the tracks into a straight 'five-a-side' format indicated that the band was focusing more on the rock element of their 'Celtic Rock' sound. Side one (culminating with 'Stowaway') was the more Irish sounding of the collection. With side two ('New York Wakes' to 'A Lifetime To Pay'), the stylings are more American-centric.

Traditional elements remained, of course, but the overall sound has the electric guitar very much as the focal point of the album. To my ears, *Aliens* has too much Fean and not enough of the multi-instrumental strengths of Lockhart and O'Connor. When these elements are more present, the album is the stronger as a result; a view to which Carr subscribes:

> I think *Aliens* fell between two stools and it could have been a lot stronger, but part of the problem was we played down the traditional instrumentation that was such a key part of the band's formula. It felt like a rush job, and we were even recycling old ideas.

The cover was, of course, another O'Connor production. The designer expounded upon his vision:

> *Aliens* was originally going to have a gloss black and white cover in a very late 19th century, old American style, with coloured badges overlaid. Inside, the inner bag would have been in full colour, with the Celtic swirls on our faces. I really wanted that strong contrast of black and white on the outside and colour on the inside, which would have been quite unpredictable and cool, but it didn't get the vote. The band thought that as we were paying so much for the printing, we may as well go full colour on the outer sleeve as well.
>
> All of the Celtic motif slides I'd created for *The Book of Invasions* were reused to project onto the band's faces. I wanted the guys to look a little run down, possibly a little gypsy-like and anonymous, to fit the theme of newly arrived immigrants. So I bought a pile of clothes for us to wear for the photo session with Ian Finlay; I crumpled them up, tied them with tape and sprayed them with metallic car spray paint. The boys seemed a bit reticent to wear them, but they looked great.

The front cover image has the air of the album images created by the design group Hipgnosis. The band is shown from the forehead down to a dark chest level, with the band and album title legend covering their eyes, making them both familiar and anonymous. In keeping with the fashion of the time, the facial hair is in retreat. Left to right, it's Carr, Devlin, Fean, Lockhart, and O'Connor. And we know this because the band's signatures are superimposed on the darkness in red. Another useful aspect was the inclusion of all the song lyrics on the inner sleeve. Aliens marked the final collaboration between the band and O'Duffy. Devlin holds a high opinion of the producers' skills:

> My theory that Alan O'Duffy produced our best albums holds a lot of water with *Aliens*. It was another great piece of work, on which we probably played better than at any other time. In many ways, it's one of my favourite album of songs.

Lockhart concurs:

> Alan had a great pair of ears and, although we sometimes felt that his productions lacked the bite that we got from other producers, he was more sensitive to what we were about musically, and was brilliant with layered vocal harmonies. Our natural emphasis was on keeping things basic and rocky, while Alan had a more symphonic vision of our music and was prepared to leave more sonic space between the instruments than some others might have allowed.

The difference in sound between albums two and three of the trilogy emphasises Lockhart's point. But more of that later. The 'O'Duffy Sound', as characterised by *The Táin*, *The Book of Invasions,* and *Aliens,* presents the band in their best sonic light, playing to their skills as instrumentalists, arrangers, composers, and vocalists.

'Before the Storm' (0.45)
This is an atmospheric, scene-setting instrumental. The sound of waves are heard, then two ships horns communicating with each other, one near, one far away, like whale-song. In all likelihood, these are taken from a sound effects record. A low, sustained organ note replaces the 'whales' and distant, 'violined' guitar appears, playing the opening phrase of what will later become 'Exiles'. The music finishes, there is the sound of waves again, and then 'The Wrath of the Rain' crashes in…

'The Wrath of the Rain' (2.54)
Devlin commented on the album's opening song:

> In 'The Wrath of the Rain' we're asking where the sons of those people might be…The track might sound Lizzy-esque to some people, but what we were actually trying to do was imitate the Steve Miller Band, which goes to show how the best-laid plans sometimes work out.

I have never considered the Steve Miller Band as a strong influence in this track. And listening again, and trying to crowbar any similarities together, I am still struggling. Thin Lizzy, however? Certainly, both the harmonised electric guitars and the relentless shuffle rhythm bring to mind the four-piece rockers. It's also not too much of a stretch to imagine Lynott's soulful singing giving voice to the excellent lyrics: 'Ragged and rough in those sepia pages, tear-streaked and fearful, alone. They were caught in the flash of the curious camera, a number, a name do you know where they've gone? They came with the faces of innocents and they left with the bodies of men, they were out on the run, they were fleeing the wrath of the rain'.

'The Wrath of the Rain' is a straight-down-the-line, shuffle rocker. It's melodic, well-written and played, and foot-tappingly engaging, but once you've heard the first verse, the rest of the song unfurls in a very similar fashion. There's no mandolin, concertina, or fiddle to illuminate the lyrical theme; the Irish, having left their homeland in desperate times, have now established an unfamiliar life for themselves in America. Guitar, bass, organ, and drums dominate to the extent that it sounds like the band have the US market firmly in their sights right from the off.

A more interesting approach would have been to introduce the rock instrumentation gradually, to meld the 'old' and 'new' musical cultures. For example, after the full-on electric introduction, the first verse could have used purely acoustic instruments; in the second, we could have the introduction of bass, drums and electric guitar, and by the time the third verse swings around, the song is in full rock mode.

A mid-song instrumental has pleasingly harmonised guitar phrases from the introduction repeatedly used, whilst way back in the mix, there are hints of flute in the response sections, before the final verse. Fean has a familiar-sounding, fourteen-bar end-of-song solo just after Devlin's clunky 'Yes, we are!' and the track comes to an abrupt end.

'The Wrath of the Rain' is positive, bouncy, and uplifting, but it sounds like a mid-side track rather than a dramatic opening song to match the quality of, for example, 'Trouble (With a Capital T)'. Carr's lyrics are poetic throughout; highlights include 'Deadbeat with drifting they scrambled ashore, and they ran from the spell of the sea', and 'Where have they gone to, those faded faces, those fierce moustachioed men? The women and boys and their tattered belongings, what has become of the loss and the pain?'

The music, good though it is, isn't as good as it should be, especially for those anticipating a continuance of the quality levels established with *The Book of Invasions*.

'Speed the Plough' (3.31)

This track is an example of the band reusing old ideas rather than writing a brand new album of specific, focused material. The song was originally intended to be a part of 'The Tain'.

Devlin commented:

> We occasionally played 'Speed the Plough' live from 1973. It always had a cool rhythm and the harmonies added a unique twist. It's mainly Jim's music with Eamon's lyrics. For some reason we had trouble in settling on a tempo. But when we came to record *Aliens*, it suddenly felt right within this new frame, so we locked it down and fell in love with it.

'Speed the Plough' has much going for it (a nicely funky underlying groove, a catchy chorus, excellent lead and backing vocals), but there are some negatives. The song is built around a frequently reoccurring, repetitive electric guitar refrain. There is an unimaginative structure of verse/chorus/verse/ chorus/instrumental/repeat verse/ two choruses to end. This is played out against a backdrop of unchanging dynamics and texture, with the overall feeling being one of a decent enough set of ideas not having had a great deal of creativity applied to them.

There are, again, some memorable lyrics ('I counted lines on her pretty face, and felt the tears she cried, her cheeks were bleached as white as snow as she kissed me goodbye'), but that said, verse three is an uninspiring repeat of the first verse.

The electric mandolin has a significant part to play, chipping in with plenty of arpeggios and as a foil for the mid-song guitar solo. But, here again, an opportunity to bring in the violin or concertina to broaden the instrumental section would have yielded more interesting results. Musically, the best parts of the song are in the chorus, where the layered vocal harmonies are exceptional, and Fean's singing throughout the song has a fantastic tone. But overall, 'Speed the Plough' is a notch down from what was expected. The song comes to a tight halt after two final choruses halfway through one of the guitar phrases.

'Speed the Plough' backed with 'Bridge From Heart to Heart' and 'Red River Rock (Live)' was issued as a single in the UK on 23 June 1978. The two 'B-side' songs would later appear on the 2013 singles compilation *Biography*.

'Sure the Boy was Green' (4.39)

'The Morrison's Jig' is the traditional tune which is threaded through much of 'Sure the Boy Was Green'. 'And the award for 'Sword of Light Two' goes to...'. Well, not quite, but 'Sure the Boy Was Green' is the first song on Aliens to sound like the band's collective heart is truly in it. There is a real, driving energy to the track. The combination of bubbling bass, distorted guitar, high-pitched mandolin, enthusiastic flute, and inventive drumming makes this up-tempo shuffle rocker a strong contender for 'Song of the Album'.

The chorus is wonderful, full of energy and passion, with Fean throwing excerpts from the source material into the mix. Everyone is at the top of their game here. The superb lyrics ('He was only a mad moonlighter, dancing by the sea, envying nobody, chasing shadows crazy and free') are delivered with spirit by Fean. There's plenty of traditional instrumentation amongst all the rock band backing, and the chorus vocals are, again, first-class.

Another mid-song guitar solo (that's three in a row, lads…) leads into the bridge section (2.15), with more well-harmonised vocals ('Ooh, torch-bearing lady, see this guy he's in love with you. Ooh dream-selling lady, he's in need, you'd better come through') precedes another chorus. The final section of vocals has verses one and two back for another go, and the last chorus leads into an apparent coda section with the jig riff blazing away on guitar as the song fades away.

But that's not all there is. Mandolin and acoustic guitar slide back in, briefly, playing another version of 'The Morrison's Jig' before fading away again. It's refreshing to hear the acoustic music in amongst all the rock instrumentation; sadly, there isn't enough of it, either here, or across the entire album.

'Sure the Boy Was Green' was issued as part of the 'Tour-A-Loor-A-Loor-A-Loor-A' EP (along with 'Red River Rock (Live)', 'Trouble (With a Capital T), and 'Bridge From Hear to Heart') in Ireland on 28 July 1978.

'Come Summer' (3.24)

Referencing the traditional song 'Tiocfaidh An Samhradh' ('Summer Will Come') in the chorus sections, 'Come Summer' is another guitar-led, mid-paced groover. There is a poppy feel to the opening syncopated riff, which grooves away over a 6/8 time signature before coming to an abrupt stop, leaving space for an isolated flute solo. The rock backing returns with an additional flute playing a harmony line over the chord progression. This will later be used as the basis for the chorus.

There are some neat touches to the verse. Devlin sings the first line alone ('There's a fire that you can't see burning'), only for his response phrase ('There's a voice on the wind, and it's telling who's sinned') to be joined by a lower register vocal. This idea is repeated throughout the verse before the final lines ('There's a different man, time's going to make you a different man') where, once again, the harmony vocals work superbly well, building into the chorus, which Devlin has to himself. Here the flute weaves its way around the vocal melody before the song moves immediately into its second verse.

Following the second chorus, the instrumental section is led by the flute over the verse chord sequence, just leaving time for a final chorus with the song coming to a tight end. Whilst the emphasis on the flute is a welcome addition to this enjoyably melodic song, the largely altered dynamics and texture makes 'Come Summer' less involving than it could have been.

If, for example, acoustic guitar and mandolin (carrying over from the play-out of 'Sure the Boy Was Green') was included as part of the arrangement here, it would have given the album's theme of exile a greater cohesion. Similarly, the addition of fiddle or concertina to the mix would have added to the musical variety and enjoyment of the song.

'Stowaway' (3.34)

There's a real change of mood and pace with this Devlin composition. Atmospheric electric and acoustic guitar arpeggios are soon joined by a strummed steel strung guitar. A vast amount of reverberation is included, together with a pulsing bass and percussion rhythm, which provide a ghostly, effective introduction.

The vocals have a haunting, ethereal sound to them. Producer O'Duffy has skilfully added a reversed reverberation effect where the 'tail' of the note is heard before the word itself is sung: 'I'm just a stowaway, adrift on the sea.' This effect is dispensed with for the chorus ('I didn't build the ship, I didn't cry the sea. I'm just a stowaway, don't go bothering me') as archetypal AOR guitar power chords scythe through the backing instrumentation.

The second verse and chorus follow a similar pattern, with the addition of some stylish keyboard phrases, and a delay effect added to the guitar chords. At 1.37, the bridge section has a curiously poppy, Beatles-esque quality to it before a soulful guitar solo (other instruments are available. Follow me for more arrangement tips!) The third verse and chorus have the song's best lyrics: 'I'm just a memory, a dream and a sigh. But sighs can drift away and dreams can tell a lie. I'm just a memory and memories never die'. This final line is repeated as another guitar solo hoves into view and the song fades away on its galloping rhythm.

'Stowaway' is another good, but not great, song with too much guitar in the mix. There's a sameness to the five songs on what was side one, with the exception of 'Sure the Boy Was Green', which means the compositions only reveal their individual gifts after repeated listenings. Fortunately, the five tracks on side two are more diverse and rewarding.

'New York Wakes' (4.04)

The song title was the term given to emigrant farewell parties held in Ireland. The opening riff is played in unison on overdriven electric guitar and flute is borrowed from 'The Fox Hunter's Jig'. This traditional tune (in 9/8 time) is rearranged into 4/4 for this first-class, melodic rocker.

Rapid fire drums bring in the song proper, with Devlin giving fine voice to the evocative lyrics, highlights of which include; 'We built a city out of junkyard alleys and landscape valleys where the dead men sleep', 'And set your face against the rush of feet and the sidewalk heat and the café light', and, best of all in explaining the mindset of the city that never sleeps, 'No one here is going to take the time to read your mind or save your soul.'

The pre-chorus and chorus are just superb, combining a strong melody with more great words and an uplifting feel. There's energy, attitude and passion here by the bucket load. Flute and mandolin dance away in the background of this section. Again, effective backing vocals (which includes O'Duffy singing the falsetto line) add to the effect, and then we're back into the full-blooded version of the introduction again for the second verse. The second pre-chorus has a neat throwback to *Danceball Sweethearts* with the reference to the 'Night-time boys (and Broadway jigs)', which 'helped keep your footwork neat'.

At 2.12, a reflective instrumental section begins. This takes the underlying verse chord progression and slows it to a half-time tempo with some atmospheric, descending guitar arpeggios and a single, sustained feedback note. Then the music begins to build and build, with mandolin, flute and bass interweaving their melodies as the drums increase in presence and volume, reflecting the hustle and bustle of the city. Then we are back into the energy and drive for the third verse and chorus, which is a repeat of the first set.

'New York Wakes' ends by reprising the introduction with the full-band backing, the final note being more sustained guitar feedback which leads immediately into…

'Exiles' (3.12)

The album's only true instrumental is a fine follow-up to 'Fantasia'. Interestingly (I'll be the judge of that), it was placed in the exact same place on the album in the days of vinyl: side two, track two.

'Exiles' is based around two traditional tunes: 'Fill, Fill A Ruin O' ('Return, return, my dearest') with the secondary melody taken from the third line of the traditional song 'Carrickfergus' ('But the sea is wide and I cannot swim over, neither have I the wings to fly...').

In response to the closing guitar note of 'New York Wakes', the ship horn from 'Before the Storm' reappears, as does the guitar's 'violin' introduction. Then this relaxed and reflective instrumental begins playing to all of the band's instrumental strengths simultaneously. Fean has the main theme ('Fill, Fill A Ruin O') and plays with an absolutely exquisite guitar tone, whilst in the background additional atmosphere is provided by plucked violin. When the melody transfers to the flute, the contrast is stunning. In the background, we hear violin, acoustic guitar, bass and drums providing a steady but never dull backdrop, their parts full of inventiveness and tasteful playing.

But really, 'Exiles' is a showcase for Fean's melodic skill and tasteful phrasing ability, as he occasionally plays in harmony with himself. It is simply a beautiful piece of music, expertly arranged, superbly executed.

'Exiles' (paired with 'Speed the Plough') was issued as a single in Ireland on 24 November 1977.

'Second Avenue' (4.01)

'Second Avenue' describes the teeming life of New York as yet another emigrant-carrying ship arrives in harbour. Lockhart claims that any similarities between it and 'Teacher' by Jethro Tull (from their 1970 album *Benefit*) to be '…pure coincidence, Maybe it was a subliminal tribute.'

Where I struggled to find the Steve Miller Band inspiration behind 'The Wrath of the Rain', there's no such problem with 'Second Avenue'. The central guitar riff to this track is rhythmically identical to the older song, the only difference being the key signature: Tull's track is in A major, 'Second Avenue' is in D major. The good news is that they are both great numbers.

'Second Avenue' opens with a steadily rhythmic and very pretty chord arpeggio sequence on acoustic and electric guitar, before the band hit the ground, if not running, then certainly walking at a determined pace with this mid-tempo melodic rocker. Devlin's vocals are relatively laid-back against the solid groove, with his bass having plenty of space within the arrangement to add some suitably funky lines. These act well in conjunction with the neat mandolin chord work.

The pre-chorus and chorus are mini-masterclasses of power, melody and arrangement: 'So tell the people, the future's on its way, that's what the papers say'. A counterpoint melody on flute leads into a short instrumental. The flute continues in the second verse, which again brings to mind comparisons with Ian Anderson's playing on many Tull songs. Let's call it another coincidence.

At 2.14, a distinctive guitar solo is blended with interjections on flute, and interesting percussive touches before the final lyrics: 'All along the darkened streets the news is spreading fast, the dancers are all leaving and the crowd is still, the music's stopped at last'. Repeated choruses feature the short, single-bar traditional motif. In this coda section, it takes on a longer form to become a fading play-out, which transfers to O'Connor playing 'The Morrison's Jig' in isolation on the concertina to close.

'Ghosts' (3.33)

Originally called 'A Dancer After Dreams', 'Ghosts' is the album's big, no, make that *huge*, ballad. Built around the traditional tune 'An Chuilfhionn' and sung by Fean, it is a song *par excellence*. From the evocative keyboard introduction, through the gently hypnotic acoustic guitar-led rhythm section, to Fean's occasionally falsetto vocals, 'Ghosts' is magnificent.

Understated throughout, it's refreshing to hear a soaring violin take the place of the electric guitar for the post-second verse instrumental section. There's no huge dynamic rise and fall here; 'Ghosts' is a simple, but highly effective track, the arrangement of which gives plenty of space for the lyrics (just three verses, no choruses, no bridge section) to shine: 'I lived alone without you, shadows on my wall, ghosts in my looking glass and voices in the hall.', and 'Mine was just a foolish heart, couldn't fake a smile, thought I'd find deliverance down another mile'. The final line ('The love I find in dreams') is repeated, as has been the case with the preceding verses, and the song draws to a natural end. Stunning. Just stunning.

'A Lifetime to Pay' (4.05)

Continuing the now well-established tradition of ending an album with an uplifting rocker, 'A Lifetime to Pay' is this album's hardest-hitting track. In direct contrast to the calm waters of 'Ghosts', it starts fast and heavy and doesn't let up one iota throughout its four-minute duration.

Beginning with brutal power chords, and some excellent slide guitar work which is imitated by the flute on the repeat phrase, the song soon launches into an up-tempo aural assault where subtlety is thrown out of the window, and the band revert to all-out rock mode again. Original titles for the song, originally conceived three years previously, included 'Nothing to Say' and 'The American Way', and it's clear that the focus is firmly back on the United States: 'So this is your day, look around you, you've made it at last the American way.'

The pulverising pace and rhythm have an almost punk-ethos running through them, the single acknowledgement of the band's wide-ranging talents being the manic flute interjections throughout the track. The only change of feel to the song comes at 1.45, where the music slips into half-time tempo for a bridge section: 'And all you've ever wanted was a place in the sun, a place in the sun…'. A rapid flurry of triplet guitar harmonics signifies a return to the previous pace and energy, and, sadly, a repeat of the second verse.

This leads into a lengthy coda section (2.56) which starts with a reprise of the introduction before a steadily building crescendo of a chord progression, driven along by aggressive drumming. The organ chords climb and climb, high-pitched guitar swings in, and the song grinds to a somewhat messy stop, ending with a grunting 'fall-off' note on the bass. In retrospect, this driving, powerful end section sounds like it should have gone into a long fade, with the relentless power-chord progression pounding away into the distance, but clearly, the crescendo of volume and layering of keyboard harmonies sounded better coming to a specific finish – just a thought.

'A Lifetime to Pay' is savage lyrically, almost Pink Floyd-esque in its apparent bile ('You've worked for it all, had your back to the wall, now it's free for all, the American Way') and highly aggressive tone; the musical equivalent of a stressful day in a hot city. If the band's next producer had got his hands on this, it would have been close to an all-out heavy metal stampede. As it is, O'Duffy's sense of control and balance ensures this fine rocker ends *Aliens* on a high note.

The Man Who Built America (1978)

Personnel:
Eamon Carr: drums
Barry Devlin: bass, vocals
John Fean: guitars, vocals
Jim Lockhart: keyboards, flute, whistles, vocals
Charles O'Connor: fiddle, mandolin, concertina, vocals
Recorded at Advison Studios, London
Produced by Steve Katz
Engineered by Dee O'Doherty
Assistant Engineer: Nick Walker
All tracks composed/arranged by Carr, Devlin, Fean, O'Connor, and Lockhart
Released on 27 October 1978
Issued on Oats Records in Ireland (M0017), DJM in the UK (DJF 20546 – 19 January 1979), and DJM DJLPA-20 (USA)

Horslips toured America and the United Kingdom to promote *Aliens* in late 1977. In November, 'Exiles' / 'Speed the Plough' was released as a single in Ireland, staying on the charts for seven weeks and reaching number nine. The tour continued in Germany, and the band rounded off a successful year with an attendance record-breaking series of concerts in Ireland, which continued into early 1978.

In February, Horslips jetted off to the States again, with 'Sure the Boy Was Green' / 'Exiles' being released as a single there. The American tour extended until May 1978 and was followed with another Irish tour. The band was introduced to a wider rock audience when they were 'special guests' (support act) for Thin Lizzy, who were playing Wembley Empire Pool for two nights as part of their *Live And Dangerous* tour.

On 23 June, 'Speed the Plough' was issued as a single in the UK, with a live cover of Johnny & The Hurricanes' 1959 hit instrumental 'Red River Rock' and 'Bridge From Heart to Heart' on the B-side. June, July, and August saw the band touring in Ireland again, whilst rehearing songs for their next album. On 28 July, the band released another 'Ireland only' record, an EP featuring 'Sure the Boy Was Green', 'Red River Rock', 'Trouble (With a Capital T), and 'Bridge From Heart to Heart'. It peaked at number nine in the chart.

Recording sessions for what would become *The Man Who Built America* began at Lombard Studios in Dublin. Technical problems with the studio equipment meant that the sessions were abandoned, and the project moved to Advison Studios in London, with the new album finally being released at the end of October. The Man *Who Built America* is both a continuation of, and a diversion from, what had been before. As Devlin said:

> We felt there was a legitimate reason to continue the migration theme, which is how *The Man Who Built America* came about. It was originally going to

be titled 'The Wheels Of The World', a title which had been hanging in the air since we included the phrase in 'The Power and the Glory' and we saw it had additional merit. *Aliens* and *The Man Who Built America* were held together in how they looked and felt by the remnants of a trilogy idea, to follow *The Book of Invasions*. When we finished *Invasions* we all agreed that this approach worked for us, in that this was what Horslips was always about, and that there were other tales of migrations to deal with.

So, conceptually, at least, there was a continuity of theme. However, the change of producer from Alan O'Duffy, who had achieved such peerless results with the previous two albums, to Steve Katz was significant, and not in a good way. Out goes subtlety and carefully conceived arrangements; in comes a big, brash, American 'stadium rock' sound. If *Aliens* featured a lot of Fean, *The Man Who Built America* has too much.

The Man Who Built America is the aural equivalent of being stuck in Times Square, New York City, on a busy summer's day, unable to find your way out. To extend the metaphor further, possibly to breaking point, the overall sound is nearly all concrete, steel, and city noise, with very little space for greenery. Where the traditional roots break through, they are as welcome as ever. However, they are soon swamped with the blitz of guitar-led 'rawk'. That's not to say *The Man Who Built America* is a bad album – it really isn't. The ten songs are, in the main, as strong, involving, and melodic as ever, but there's so little space for the music to breathe amongst all the distortion and reverberation. If Alan O'Duffy had been retained as producer, the end result would have been very different and, almost certainly, more pleasurable to listen to. This isn't just my view, as Fean opined:

I was in favour of a bigger guitar sound, and with tracks like 'I'll Be Waiting' and 'Loneliness', that big sound was our new foundation. But in achieving that, we lost something else along the way; the traditional instrumentation that was Horslips' original trademark. I think we were so focused on achieving that 'stadium rock' sheen that we overlooked getting the balance of the instrumentation right.

Good point well made; not broken, don't fix it, and so forth. The fact that a trilogy of albums was envisaged, then the continued involvement of O'Duffy would have brought a uniformity of sound to the projects. If the band then decided to pursue a different approach and producer, the album after the completion of the trilogy would have been the time to make a change. The desire for significant success in America seems to have overridden these considerations. Carr concurs:

More than at any other time, I felt a style shift. I wasn't happy with the direction of *The Man Who Built America* and it's no one person's fault. I bought into having Steve Katz as the producer. I was there when we were figuring out our drum sound and I roundly endorsed a third part of the loose trilogy idea. But I envisioned more of a sepia-toned roots approach than embracing stadium rock. There would be electric stuff on it as well as concertina and fiddle, and probably leaning more towards John Mellencamp. We just didn't have that collective vision.

O'Connor is more supportive of the sound of the album:

The production does sound American, and that's precisely what we expected from Steve Katz, or we'd have asked Alan to stay on. Steve got the most exciting guitar, bass, and drum sounds we ever had on an album. It sounds very live, and that was one of the things we agreed had been lacking. As for the traditional elements, I thought they were woven in very nicely and in a credible way, so as not to feel like pastiche. The album is probably a little patchy in places, but the good stuff made up for that in spades.

The cover, another O'Connor production, was, like the album, very angular, full of darkness and primary colours. He actually designed two sleeves; the one for the Irish market reprised the Celtic motif from *The Book of Invasions* to reinforce the fact that this was the third of the trilogy. The other version was used where the album appeared elsewhere. He described the creative process;

Both of them shared the device of the stripes from the US flag. It was a request from DJM Records and there was a bit of hedge-betting going on, but ultimately it confused some people. The default international version had a grainy picture of a helicopter shining its light on a group of fugitives from a scene in a detective book. There was a crime aspect to it, as opposed to emphasising Barry's idea of the Irish exiles. I saw a close-up of the Statue of Liberty's face and I suddenly realised it looked amazingly like Elvis Presley. Now, what sense that made I don't know, but somewhere in my mind, I could see that having this heavily pasteurised image of that face on the cover might lend itself to a wide range of interpretation. We went to Ardmore Studios in Bray with Ian Finlay for the back cover photo of the band, and made an 'alley' out of Styrofoam, with studio lighting back and front. I wanted to give the impression of gangsters sneaking around a back alley. It was very moody.

Included in the inner lyric sleeve was a quotation in Gaelic from the Irish poet Mairtin O'Ireain (1910 – 1988). It translates as: 'We bade farewell to land, to shore, since fate forced us to go'. If 'land' and 'shore' are the traditional instruments and arrangements, and 'fate' is the dream of cracking the American market with a stadium rock sound, then the quotation is very

apposite. In reality, of course, it is a reminder that this album follows the themes of *The Book of Invasions* and *Aliens. The Man Who Built America* was the first Horslips album not to feature a purely instrumental track, and the ten songs continued the style established with *Aliens;* concise compositions but this time with an even greater rock, sorry, rawk bias. There is plenty of melody, and memorable moments abound, but as a cohesive piece of work, it is the weakest of the three, and, in retrospect, was the beginning of the end for the band.

The promotional strap-line from DJM Records for the album was 'Horslips – Drawing from the past, Shaping rock's future.' Hmmm. 'Drawing from the past' is certainly true; not so much 'Shaping rock's future' as 'Imitating bigger fish already swimming in a gigantic pond.' I agree that wouldn't look great on an advertising hoarding.

'Loneliness' (4.18)

A strident church organ melody opens the first track, with distorted guitar, bass, and drums kicking in to create a permanently up-tempo rocker. This immediately establishes the album's sound: big, brash, lacking in subtlety or, to deploy a cliché, American. O'Connor is correct in his assertion that Katz succeeded in capturing the most 'alive' sounding version of Horslips in the studio. It's all very 'in your face', or perhaps, more appropriately, 'in your ears'.

Fean's lead vocal carries the regretful lyrics ('Remember the way it started, leaves on a stream, seasons to dream, when we were younger we were home') with style, and there are some effective backing harmonies. The chorus is strong and memorably melodic, and the overall effect is of a powerful, foot-tapping four-to-the-floor track.

After the second chorus, O'Connor comes into his own for the instrumental section (2.47 – 3.09) with a spectacular fiddle solo, as the organ moves further forward in the mix with a reprise of the introductory tune. A repeat of the pre-chorus ('Lady, come home, I want to find you on your own. I'm so alone, and I need you, yes I need you') leads into two further choruses. The coda section continues the same chord progression with a buzzy, chorus guitar melody riding high in the mix, as the song comes to an end with a sustained organ chord.

'Loneliness' (paired with 'Homesick') was released as a single in the UK on 2 June 1979.

'Tonight (You're With Me)' (3.23)

This starts with an a capella version of the chorus, the lead unison vocals in the right stereo channel balanced with the harmony vocals in the left. A rocking shuffle rhythm backing kicks in beneath some sub-optimal first verse lyrics: 'Tomorrow's the day, I gotta go, I hate to leave you, but you know I can't stay, I'm away'. Sound-wise it's all distorted, power-chord guitar, bass, and drums.

The pre-chorus is better both musically and lyrically: 'Wherever dreams are sold, you'll find me spending all my money and time on a pot of gold, but like the rainbow it's never-ending.' The chorus has some tasty 'Lizzy-esque' guitar harmonies. A second unexceptional verse features some nice electric piano added in and synth joins for the pre-chorus, which builds the musical texture up well. A second chorus leads into an instrumental section (1.41 – 2.06), the first part of which definitely brings 'the Boys' very much back to 'the town'. At 1.47 'the boys' suddenly realise they are in fact, Horslips, and the synth brings in the 'Lark in the Morning' jig to great effect. This is harmonised with a further synth line. The third verse, which thinks the first verse was so good it's worth repeating, then appears – it's wrong.

The final chorus brings in the 'Lark in the Morning' jig again, with a long, distorted power chord fading away, allowing the vocal harmonies to shine again in another a-cappella chorus. A sudden key change with band and jig at full pelt keeps the interest level high, but weirdly the song comes to an 'early Beatles' style vocal end rather than fading away on a high energy play out. The song would have been all the better for a continuation of the 'Lark in the Morning' jig following the key modulation. As a result, the end is neither pop, nor rock – nor much good.

'I'll Be Waiting' (6.29)

The first of the album's two 'big ballads', 'I'll Be Waiting' once again showcases Fean's fine vocals and emotive solo talents. It's an excellent song that is almost entirely spoilt by the 'stadium rock' production.

Using the traditional tune 'Dingle Bay' as the musical DNA of the chorus, the lyrics had two sources of inspiration. The first was a young lady who was employed at the Great Northern Hotel in Bundoran, where the band were staying, who was planning to emigrate. The second was the novel *And Quiet Flows The Don* by the Russian writer Mikhail Sholokov (1905 – 1984). The book's heroine, Aksinia, changed nationality in Carr's mind to become the Irish girl who is left behind, hence the chorus lines, 'So take your time, don't you worry, I'll be waiting, you know I'll be waiting.'

The slow, walking tempo, country-style piano and organ, strummed acoustic guitar, subtle bass, and drums provide a tasteful backdrop to the evocative lyrics: 'I sat on the doorstep and watched her slowly walk away' and in the pre-chorus: 'So what's the matter with indifference, it's just an easy way to kill the pain'. Fean handles the vocal duties with style and emotion, but the entire endeavour is swamped, nay drowned, in reverb. The subtleties of the composition and arrangement are swept away in a vast, canyon-like soundscape. This doesn't *ruin* the track, 'I'll Be Waiting' is too good for that, but it does lessen the enjoyment to a significant degree. The vocals are not far enough forward in the mix, and whilst the backing vocals in the chorus are well-sung, there is a mushy feel to the sound, which really doesn't work at all. The individual elements fail to stand out, there's little light and shade, and after a while, it becomes hard work to listen effectively to everything that's going on.

Given the poetic lyrics, especially in the second verse ('Don't want to be a ploughboy, seen my father break his back that way, I'm not a dreamer, I'm a builder, at least that's what the voices say'), a cleaner, 'drier' mix would have made the combination of words and music so much more effective. Meanwhile, vocals boom, cymbals splash, and everything sounds unnecessarily big for what is, in reality, an intimate, reflective composition.

'I'll Be Waiting' is a prime example of W.W.O'D.D. syndrome. What would O'Duffy do? In his hands, I imagine the sound to have remained expansive, but with the space around the notes, chords, and instruments being given room to breathe. 'Ghosts' springs to mind instantly as a point of comparison; a similarly epic, beautiful slow song where the vocals were allowed to gently dominate, and the band provide a superb backing, with plenty of variation in both instrumental texture and dynamics. Katz's production is much more a case of everything. All the time.

At 2.35, Fean has his first significant solo; it's highly melodic, well structured and fits the music well, but if this section had been given over to a soaring violin interlude or an evocative flute, the power of the song would have been increased and the contrasts would be heightened compared to the relentless instrumental mix we have here.

At 3.17, another pre-chorus and chorus indicate that the track is in its final stages. However, the play-out guitar solo after the repeated choruses (4.03 – 6.29) goes on for too long – *much* too long. It's not Fean's soloing *per se*, he is a fine guitarist who plays for the song, and nothing about what he creates here sounds wrong, self-indulgent, or out of place. The problem is the continual aural assault of the same instruments, volume, and dynamics being overly used. And it's such a shame; 'I'll Be Waiting' is a great ballad, but under Katz's direction, it becomes a lumbering, bloated, overly long, and sadly deflating dirge.

The definitive version appears on 2011's *Horslips and the Ulster Orchestra* live album. Here, the orchestral arrangements by Brian Byrne really bring the power and scope of this epic song into sharp focus in a way that Katz's production singularly fails to do.

'If it Takes All Night' (3.35)

'If it Takes All Night' takes the traditional melody 'Limerick Rake' and subtly integrates it into the chorus of this taut little pop-rocker. The opening guitar riff is joined by bass and flute, before a secondary (chorus) melody increases the tension along with some thunderous drums, which is followed by a more relaxed verse backing.

Strangely, Devlin's vocal sounds like he has been recorded down a telephone line and the lyrics deserve better: 'I was only a passer-by, I couldn't get involved, but you seemed so lost, so off your course, I ran to help you when you called. You were only a little child, a face behind the wall, you were compromised, not worldly wise, you saw and heard and felt it all.'

Unfortunately, the heavier chorus goes delving deep into the drawer of clichés and comes up with 'If it takes all night, I'm going to love you and make it right' – oh dear. This was the kind of stereotypical rubbish that bands like Kiss were purveying. Carr can do so much better than this. Again the degree of reverb added to the backing vocals spoils the overall effect, and the welcome inclusion of some traditional instrumentation does not standout as a feature.

An instrumental section, beginning two minutes into the song, is played out over the verse chord progression with plenty of harmonised electric guitars and, somewhere in the background, some tin whistle makes a brief appearance. The third verse commits the cardinal sin of rerunning the first one, in pretty much the same way I keep mentioning it each time it happens. Why do this? Carr has set up an interesting story of an unnamed character in the second verse ('You lost your heart when you found your way to the neon side of town. Now it's no surprise to realise the friends you've made have let you down') and then it's just…abandoned.

Repeated choruses drive the song to a conclusion, with the introduction being repeated as a coda, this unexceptional number ending on a single sustained chord. 'If it Takes All Night' is Horslips playing at being a very average American rock band (with, admittedly, some interesting if muffled textural additions) and sadly succeeding. If this song was a car on a long journey, it would surely drive into a town called 'Filler' and park up for the night.

'Green Star Liner' (3.26)

The Green Star Line was an American steamship shipping line created in 1919 and operated until 1923. It was established by Irish businessmen as a response to a campaign urging Americans to buy ships for wealth and patriotism during and after World War I. The company title is a neat play on 'The White Star Line' of Titanic fame, which operated during the same period.

Featuring electric harpsichord (and the uncredited guest musician Tommy McCarthy on uilleann pipes), 'Green Star Liner' is the first song on the album which sounds like Horslips being Horslips. Highly melodic, skillfully arranged, and blending traditional and rock instrumentation, the fusion sound returns in this Devlin composition.

'Green Star Liner' plays more to the 'pop' side of the band's spectrum, especially with the addictive, commercial chorus. Fans of the traditional repertoire may spot 'The Eagle's Whistle' in the arrangement, and the uilleann pipe solo is a standout section. Lockhart's Baroque-style introduction (which will also feature in the accompaniment of the chorus) leads into a verse where acoustic guitar and a relaxed bass and drum backing provide some much-needed textural relief from the 'big rawk' sound, which has dominated the first four songs. There's some excellent, understated electric guitar motifs and Devlin's voice soars into the chorus, where handclaps and tambourine continue the lighter sonic feel: 'Green star liner carry me to find a shelter from the sea. Forty miles nearer, twenty times clearer, what I want to be.'

Simple in structure (verse, chorus, verse, chorus, instrumental, repeat chorus to fade), as befits the 'acoustic pop' nature of the song, it would be more satisfying for this song to have been developed and extended. A bridge section would have helped achieve this, and again another verse would have aided the story arc. But this is relatively minor criticism; 'Green Star Liner' is another excellent example of the band's ability to fuse together the traditional with the more modern and emerge with a compelling and catchy composition.

'The Man Who Built America' (4.25)

Carr was quoted in a review by Graham Lock published in the 3 February 1979 issue of *New Musical Express* saying, 'It's about the idea that people can find a new place and build it from the ground up.' The album's title track is also its best song, and the first of the collection not to be written in the first person. Released as a single in the United Kingdom on 2 June 1979 (backed with 'Long Weekend'), it was, as Devlin attested to:

> ...a sort of sequel to the theme of 'The Wrath of the Rain', specifically from the line 'I see them today in the streets of their cities, we nod to each other again'. I was following on to see what kind of America they'd built and had been built around them. Hence the golden spike where the Eastward railroad met the Westward. The golden mile was the gold-lined umbilical cord of the spacewalker with the distant Earth reflected in his visor.

Detailing the lyrics further he added:

> 'You coloured kids on the borderline...' was all about white, black and Hispanic in the Watts riots, as was 'in every precinct a golden mile', but more specifically about Robert Kennedy and Martin Luther King. And 'you kill the rich and you con the poor' was a kind of upside-down version of Republican and Democratic politics. It was a go at pretty much anything.

Swirling church organ arpeggios usher in the first verse: 'See him driving those golden nails, that hold together the silver bars, that one day gonna take us to the stars, cos he's the man who built America'. At this point, the rest of the band unleash full rawk mode. The chorus is just as melodically excellent as the preceding verses, with strong backing vocals.

Flute rides over the music for the next verses, with the chorus leading into an instrumental where Lockhart gives it his all against the powerful band backing. And then, just as things were going so well, 'it' happens again. The next verse is the first one again (admittedly backed by the full band rather than just the organ). America, and its history, are surely big enough subjects for fresh lyrics to have been included at this point. No? Just me, then. The final section gives space for a fine, suitably tortured guitar solo, before the song drives through to a tight ending after a final 'Not him, not the man who built America.'

This is a great track combining intelligent, poetic words with strong melodies and a pulversing rock accompaniment. It's also the composition where Katz's production style works the best; this is a *big* song, almost entirely devoid of subtlety, it grabs you by the ears and then hits you between the eyes, and we are all the better for the experience.

'The Man Who Built America' (backed by 'Long Weekend') was released as a single in the UK on 2 June 1979.

'Homesick' (4.02)

Opening with a repeated five-bar guitar riff, again in 4/4 time, with some nice harmony lines on the organ, 'Homesick' soon develops into another 'shuffle-a-la-Lizzy' song which has its basis in the traditional tune 'Behind the Bush in the Garden'. This is, again, an overly busy, guitar-laden, yet still effective rocker with the occasionally evocative lyrical couplet: 'Outside my room, a light is flashing so the night can never gain a hold, and in the language that the stranger doesn't know he's often easy rolled.'

The pre-chorus ('And though I'm finding it hard to smile, no need to worry for in a while') builds magnificently into the high-energy chorus ('It's alright, I was feeling kind of homesick, but that's alright.'). Flute decorates this section most effectively, but the instrumental section after the second chorus (1.44 – 2.17) doesn't capitalise on this opportunity and another guitar solo takes centre stage again.

After a further chorus, the song dips in the bridge section (2.33), where Carr seems to have taken inspiration from motivational posters. You know the sort of thing; eagles fly into sunsets over mountain ranges, tigers stare purposefully towards a distant horizon, a badger contemplates the ultimate futility of life as it attempts to cross a busy road (okay, maybe not this last one). But when you get 'Chances are for taking, fortune will smile on the boldest one…Keep on believing your time will come and you'll see it through', the mind, well *my* mind, does drift off in this direction.

Luckily things move up a substantial gear after another disappointing lyrical reprise (step forward verse two, your time has come. Again). From seemingly out of nowhere, a double-time version of 'Brian Boru's March' makes a riotous appearance in the final set of choruses, first with flute, then played in unison on the guitar. This is where the track finally sounds glorious; again, the power of a good rock song allied to the melodic muscle of the traditional tune makes the whole far greater than the sum of its individual parts.

'Long Weekend' (3.42)

...and breathe, for 'Long Weekend', the album's second ballad, is a model of restraint, space, melody, lyric, and a compelling vocal performance. Subtle, subdued electric guitar, simple bass, atmospheric drums and O'Connor's expressive singing of his own composition all contribute to a hypnotic, engrossing listen. There are some very tasty, sustained slide guitar phrases, a gentle keyboard puts in occasional appearances, and the overall effect is close to magical. Lockhart plays a soft-toned synth solo (2.19 – 3.08) which sits magnificently within the vast, reverb enhanced (this time) production. Unusually, the complete absence of any traditional Irish instrumentation doesn't make this a lesser composition, 'Long Weekend' works just fine as it is and whereas 'I'll Be Waiting' is too long, this track could bear extension.

The lyrics depict the aftermath of a short relationship: a girl 'in the cafe on the corner' who is 'sitting, waiting for him to show' and a man, 'a stranger to this city, this country, and he's got too much to do.' For the bridge sections, the music rises up to match the heartbreak of the lyrics: 'Shout she cries, if the city is dust in your eyes. Phone, she pleads, if the city is full of those street traffic sighs', and ''Write' she says 'If you're needing a friend along the way. Come back some time, I've no reason to leave, you'll know that I'll stay.'

What may appear on an initial listen to be a straightforward arrangement has a lot more going on 'under the bonnet'. The verse is a mixture of bars of 4/4 and 6/4 time, whilst the chorus alternates between 3/4 and 4/4. This beat displacement is carefully controlled and doesn't disturb the ambience of the track. Also concealed within the vocal melody is the traditional reel 'My Love is in America', elements of which appear to varying degrees throughout the track. 'Long Weekend' concludes as it began with just voice, electric guitar, and now sustained keyboard, as the music fades into a wash of echo and reverb. Superb.

'Letters From Home' (4.14)

And now, after the calm ... 'Letters From Home' is a straightforward, four-to-the-floor commercial rocker, seemingly crafted to slot into the AOR charts alongside the likes of Boston, Cheap Trick *et al.* It's a medium-speed chugger laden with plenty of melody and distorted guitars, seemingly designed to be a deliberate crowd-pleasing clap-a-long. Brisk and to the point, bereft of any significant changes of dynamic or texture, it still rocks along reasonably.

Strong backing vocals accompany the song title, Devlin is in fine lead vocal form, and there's some decent lyrics; 'Tuesday night, stalled at a red light, images linger frayed and torn like the photographs you kept in your wallet, sons and lovers reading letters from home'. Given that the chorus suggests a link to Ireland ('It's just a letter from home telling you things that are changing'), it would have presented an opportunity for some Celtic flavour to be introduced. This doesn't happen; the solo section is all distorted electric guitar comprising of phrases we've heard before.

After the instrumental, the rest of the band drop out, leaving Fean to reprise the opening riff; and then for those of you that enjoyed verse one, the band give you an early opportunity to hear it again. Boo, and indeed, hiss. After repeated choruses, the song cruises to a fade.

'Long Time Ago' (3.31)
In the same way that 'Green Star Liner' was a refreshing slice of melodic pop rock to close off what was side one, so too is 'Long Time Ago'; it's a tuneful, Beatles-esque in places, slice of greatness, with an irresistible blend of uilleann pipes, a strong groove, and foot-tapping catchiness.

The song is built around the traditional melody 'Gardai An Ri' which is present from the start, played on the uilleann pipes. The verse vocals are harmonised, the backing harmonies are excellent, and the song cruises along with a relaxed, summery feel throughout. Fean's guitar work enhances the music, every element of the song is musical and highly melodic, and the lyrics are reflective: 'We all do what we can, but I'm different to the man I was when long time ago', and 'Our lives written in sand, I can't remember what I called myself then, long time ago.'

The overall effect of 'Long Time Ago' is that of a cooling shower after a long, hot day; it is refreshing, invigorating, and a pleasure to listen to. And, after some of the disappointments of *The Man Who Built America* (yes, 'If it Takes All Night' and 'Letters From Home', I *am* looking at you), this is a welcome reminder that the band's talent for writing thoughtful lyrics, catchy songs, and wrapping the two together in a clever fusion of the old and the new is still alive and well.

Sadly this is also the last time Horslips would sound like Horslips. Their final collection of songs, with one notable exception, would not stand the test of time at all well...

Short Stories, Tall Tales (1979)

Personnel:
Eamon Carr: drums, bodrahn
Barry Devlin: bass, vocals
John Fean: guitars, vocals
Jim Lockhart: keyboards, flute
Charles O'Connor: guitars, vocals
Guest musicians:
Dec O'Doherty: Piano ('The Live You Save')
Ztak Evets: Tambourine
Recorded at Windmill Lane Studios
Produced by Steve Katz
Engineered by Dec O'Doherty
All tracks composed/arranged by Carr, Devlin, Fean, O'Connor, and Lockhart
Released on 16 November 1979
Issued on Oats Records in Ireland (M0019), Mercury Records in the UK (9100-070 – 30 November 1979), Mercury Records SRM-1-3089 in USA

The trilogy of emigration-themed, conceptual albums was now complete. It was now time to strike out for pastures new. But which pastures? And in which direction? Devin summarised the situation:

> The basis for the tension was the dividing line between the US and the UK approach. In 1978, America was still largely unmoved by the punk explosion and their charts were still full of dinosaurs. The British thing was sharp, stripped down, and exciting, but I thought it was too big a jump for us. However, by the time we had recorded *Short Stories,* we had firmly tipped our cap in favour of the British scene. There was almost a Buzzcocks feel to some of the new stuff.

The band was splitting into factions over the evergreen subject of musical direction. Whilst Devlin was favouring a continuation of the 'traditional' approach, O'Connor (somewhat surprisingly) was moving closer to the then fashionable 'new wave' sound. This is reflected in the instrumentation attached to each band member on the album sleeve. His violin, concertina, and mandolin must be gathering dust somewhere. For the first time, the Englishman's only instrument is the guitar, which he had never been credited as playing before on a Horslips studio album. In addition to this fracturing, there was a lack of unifying purpose to the new project. Initially, the band considered composing songs linked by a theme of Irish writers. O'Connor identified the problem:

> It was rare to not have a good pool of ideas for songs to choose from when approaching a new album, so when the writing didn't come easily, it really

> felt like a chore. On *Short Stories*, the well was drying up. We didn't have much material, but I chipped in with a few things that, unfortunately weren't very loved.

Yes, those would include 'Law on the Run', Ricochet Man', 'Summer's Most Wanted Girl', 'Amazing Offer', and 'Soap Opera' then? Or, put another way, half of the album. We aren't a decade away from *The Táin*, and the band now want to sound like...this? Devlin's take on the situation, and the career path of Horslips, to this point, was:

> *Happy to Meet* and *The Táin* came out of nowhere in terms of audience expectation. We didn't know what people wanted to hear; we only knew what we wanted to do. When you've done your first few albums, if the audience are with you, you've then got to keep delivering, and that's a very tough challenge. You begin to conform to your own idea of what the audience wants to hear from you, and confusion creeps in. You start questioning who or what you actually are. For the most part, every album we made until *Short Stories* was a progression on the previous one in some way. I'd love to claim there was intelligence at work, but I'm not entirely convinced, other than we were keen not to repeat ourselves. Ultimately, *Short Stories* feels like an unfinished body of music to me.

On the *Dancehall Sweethearts* DVD, Lockhart spoke about the band post *The Man Who Built America*:

> Unfortunately, by the time we started charting in *Billboard* we were getting close to being burnt out. We were working too hard for too long and it had taken its toll. Plus, at that time, the whole kind of musical landscape was shifting around us. I mean, we were playing sort of inventive, cleverly worked out stuff and within the space of like six months, inventive, cleverly worked out stuff was very, very un-hip.

Carr shares the dissatisfaction prevalent at the time:

> Charles was saying, 'I'm writing songs'. And we probably all were. This was the album where everybody brought in their stuff and it ended up like four or five solo records, like the *White Album* (the 1968 double-studio album by The Beatles). The songs are mostly good, but the recording experience was fractious and fairly unhappy. There was always the spectre hanging over it that if, by chance, one of these tracks exploded on radio, what sort of band would we then have? Would it be Charles O'Connor's Horslips? Barry Devlin's Horslips? Jim Lockhart's Horslips? This hadn't happened until around that period, and it was a situation that I don't think could have been sustained. It started on a subtle level with *Aliens* and manifested itself fully on *Short Stories*.

The almost complete absence of traditional instrumentation, or source tunes, the constant grind of the 'write, rehearse, record, release, tour' circle, and the lack of a cohesive theme or unifying challenge meant that *Short Stories* comes up, ahem, short in nearly every department. Lockhart's view was:

> In our last two years, we were listening to stuff like The Clash, Elvis Costello, and ska-reggae, but we had set ourselves up to be a particular kind of band that was light years away from all that. Our first album had been fearless, adventurous and there were no boundaries to our creativity. Now several years down the line, we found ourselves in a situation where we could no longer be as daring.

And, as if to underline the sense of ennui and frustration in the band, the album cover clearly indicated the paucity of ideas to be found within. O'Connor's design is unimaginative and just plain dull.

The band is shown in five individual Polaroid photographs, carelessly thrown onto the middle of a tarmac road. It's a tired, unexciting image, lacking in imagination, and is, therefore the perfect representation of the musical contents.

Steve Katz was retained as producer, and he cleaned up the 'stadium rock' sound, which had proved detrimental to much of The Man Who Built America. This makes *Short Stories* easier to listen to (and even enjoy in isolated places) than its predecessor. Unfortunately, this new-found relative clarity only emphasises how insipid and weak much of the new material is. Too many of the tracks produce an involuntary reaction, and the 'skip' button is quickly pressed. A few individual moments have some shine; a guitar riff here, a neat melodic phrase or a strong chorus there, some good backing vocals, or clever use of keyboards. However, taken as a whole, *Short Stories* is an album which documents a band in decline, running close to empty on ideas, and almost entirely abandoning their unique fusion style. Devlin said in a recent *The Independent* interview: 'Punk was big and we had to come to terms with the fact that we were a prog rock band.' He attributed the subsequent break up to:

> ...a combination of running out of raw material to do the thing we did, and trying to cope with our own sense that we were terrifically old and boring, and that nobody wanted to hear us anymore.

Short Stories is an aural portrait of a band in free fall, physically and creatively exhausted after a decade of constant touring, writing, and recording. This is not a new scenario for any successful group, but another factor to add into the situation was that Horslips managed everything 'in-house'. In addition to their musical contribution, each member had a role within the band's business structure, a result of their manifest determination to be masters of their own destiny, of not being held over a barrel by a record company with a contractual obligation to 'do another *Book of Invasions*'.

Eight years had taken them from *Happy to Meet* to *Short Stories*, and the difference in sound, style, and songs is astonishing. And not in a good way. I am not suggesting that a band, having found their niche, should be immutable to change, but the savage shift which ends up on this album is as significant as it is disappointing. The cleaner, clearer Katz production is a plus, and with the right degree of traditional tunes infusing the arrangements, this could have been a *much* better album. Based solely upon this release, however, Horslips could be virtually any 'turn of the decade', new wave-esque, pop rock band. Katz offered up his opinion of the project:

> The punk influence didn't really come in until *Short Stories*. When I saw them in rehearsal, it was clear that the band had split into two parties. Barry was still waving the folky flag with his writing while Charles, who one might think was the more traditionally orientated of them all, was bringing new wave sensibilities into the mix, both musically and in the way, he dressed. It made it very difficult for me, because the challenge was to take these contrasting elements and form a composite unit. Unfortunately, I don't think I succeeded, and the result was schizophrenic. This was a genuine reflection of what was going on. I was leaning towards what Barry was doing, which was what made me fall in love with the band in the first place. And I felt that the other stuff really wasn't right for Horslips. There are things I really like about the album. In retrospect, I think that if Horslips had held on to their traditional roots and taken them in a different direction, they would have eventually achieved the popularity in the US that they were aiming for, and maybe even exceeded it.

In the *BBC Radio Ulster* broadcast with Ralph McLean on 17 March 2022, Lockhart and Devlin expressed similar views as to the incoming dissolution of the band, Lockhart said:

> For a start, we were pretty washed out. We'd been working incredibly hard. Part of the thing of running a cottage industry meant that you were kind of always watching where the money was coming in and the money was going out, how you were going to keep stuff going from month to month. We were working ludicrously hard and I saw a gig sheet recently where we finished a bunch of Irish gigs, dancehall gigs, and immediately the next night, we were in Belgium or Holland and then for two weeks we were in Germany and then like two days later we were starting in the States and it was like that a lot for a couple of years. So by a combination of overwork, and I think we'd run out of road conceptually in terms of what we started doing if we were going to stick with the agenda we had set ourselves....it kind of came to a natural sort of end.

Devlin added:

> You start a band thinking you'll get to the top of Mount Ararat and, you know, beach it up there. And we knew we were halfway up the mountain. We knew we hadn't gone as far as we had hoped to. But we also knew we'd mined the seam that we had. There wasn't anything new that we could do, and we didn't fancy starting to be another kind of Horslips. For what it's worth, the Horslips that we finished up as, we felt wasn't the band that we'd started out with. I mean, not just in terms of personnel but in terms of what we liked to do and stuff and how we liked to push ourselves. We really didn't figure we could start again.

Writing on the *AllMusic* website, Stephen MacDonald describes the band's final studio album of the first part of their history particularly well; 'A calamity of an album as Horslips, desperate for widespread success, abandoned all semblance of Irish roots and churned out an album of limp, tired pop-rock.'

It is, of course, horse(lips) for courses, but I agree wholeheartedly. Whilst writing this book, it was an absolute pleasure to revisit all of the band's albums and listen to them repeatedly, back-to-back, and in greater detail than probably ever before to assist with the text. With this single exception.

'Guests of the Nation' (3.30)

'Guests of the Nation' was released as a single in Ireland on 16 October 1979, backed by 'When Night Comes'. The song title may have been taken from the 1931 short story written by Frank O'Connor (still no relation), which told of the execution of two British soldiers captured by the Irish Republican Army during the Irish War of Independence. This would fit with the band's initial idea of composing tracks around the theme of Irish writers. Lyrically, however, there is no such correlation: 'There's too much rain for drive-in movies, instead, they built a late-night rendezvous. You might get lucky, it's understood that it's up to you. There, every black dress hides a story and every story happy-ends with you. You don't believe it? It's understood that it's strictly true'.

'Guests of the Nation' is a good, mid-tempo, guitar-led pop rocker which, with the exception of Devlin's distinctive vocals, does not sound like any previous Horslips song. It's a stripped-back mix; electric guitars, bass, and drums dominate, keyboards and handclaps make appearances, but any hint of the traditional, and expected, Horslips style is absent.

Katz has cleaned up Fean's guitar tone to give a more overdriven, as opposed to overly distorted, sound. However, there's still plenty of reverb in the mix at times which muddies the overall clarity somewhat. A sustained keyboard tone is added for the second half of the verse, which is built around a straightforward I, IV, V chord sequence, the song becoming more melodic for the pre-chorus: 'So try the shuffle and see, try out the steps, 'cos the lesson's free, try the shuffle and see...'.

The chorus is terrific, catchy and memorable; there's a higher-pitched guitar arpeggio ostinato in the background, and it's played out over the introduction: 'You're guests of the nation, and you won't ever have to pay. You got a new occupation, so you can dream till the break of day. You're guests of the nation, so you can dance ... your life away.'

The next verse piles in quickly with some evocative lyrics: 'Winter brings its own surprises, winds of change to chill you through and through. And though you blame it on time, it's understood that the blame's on you. You wrap up warm and shrug your shoulders nobody needs to tell you what to do. And if it comes to the crunch you can show them a thing or two.' Another pre-chorus leads into the second chorus, and it's from this point that the ideas seem to have dried up.

There's a simple lead guitar melody, which is repeated and harmonised, reverb is increasingly added to the repeats of the title refrain, and the track fades away. If the intent was to write short, sharp, commercially aware pop-rockers, then 'Guests of the Nation' delivers. It's by far the best song of its type on the album, but it's a long way away from the invention and fusion of ideas that made the majority of songs on *The Man Who Built America* strong. With a couple of exceptions, *Short Stories* peaks straight away, and the remaining tracks have, in the main, an impressive capacity to produce soul-sapping levels of disappointment. The first offender being ...

'Law on the Run' (2.50)

It's quick, it's rocky, with plenty of guitars riffing away over the relentless drumming, and O'Connor's distinctive vocals add character, but 'Law on the Run' is, in the main, uninspired and unmemorable.

The pre-chorus (0.22 – 0.34, and again at 1.21 – 1.32) has a catchy guitar melody which mirrors the vocals. Fean throws in one of his instantly identifiable blues-based solos for the instrumental section (which is a reprise of the introduction's punchy power-chord sequence), and there's some nice 'Lizzy-esque' harmony guitar moments elsewhere in the song.

Amusingly, and obviously not intended at the time, the final chorus has the line 'Hey mister, can you tell me what I'm doing wrong?' Well, where do I begin? At least 'Law on the Run' doesn't outstay its very limited welcome...

'Unapproved Road' (3.40)

A Devlin song inspired by picking up a hitchhiker and giving them a lift to a hospital one night after a gig, 'Unapproved Road' has the air of an AC/DC-lite track (I'm talking the Bon Scott era here), with its crunching chord progression, and the swagger of the guitar riffs. This feeling soon evaporates with Devlin's vocals: 'A late encounter with the enemy on one of those crazy

August nights'. His laconic, lilting phrasing adds a level of style which lifts this mid-tempo rocker from 'nothing special' to 'it's okay'.

The pre-chorus (0.52 – 1.06) is all chiming guitars and commercially catchy melodies. This leads into the chorus which is played out over the introduction chord progression. Backing vocals and organ add more substance, whilst the final line ('And if you walk this way, you may never come home') is evocative, well-phrased, and affecting.

A shorter second verse (eight bars instead of 16) is followed by another pre-chorus and chorus, and then (and with a sense of inevitability) a distorted guitar solo. Short and to the point, Fean's playing is always effective, if occasionally predictable in his note choice and stylistic decoration, but it's another missed opportunity to introduce a contrasting instrument. We are then back into a pre-chorus and chorus, which fades with repeated 'Unapproved Road' chants.

Sadly, whilst 'Unapproved Road' is an under-achiever, it's still the second-best rocker on the album. Unfortunately, there are still seven songs to go, only two of which have any real merit. Strap yourself in; as we leave the 'Unapproved Road', it's going to be a rough ride…

'Ricochet Man' (3.20)

What starts off sounding like it will be another reasonable attempt at a 'Horslips 2.0' commercial rock song with a heavy, rolling guitar riff, descends into a farce twelve seconds in, with some frankly laughable lyrics sung by O'Connor: 'Automatic lovers got deep penetration. She'll crack you wide open with full investigation.' Charles! What. Are. You. Talking. About?

The chorus ('I'm your rebound lover, your ricochet man') is played out over a quasi-reggae backing. Make no bones about it; this is dreadful. Whilst the brief for writing this book is to be the enthusiastic fan who retains their critical faculties, 'Ricochet Man' is one of the worst songs the band ever recorded. And it gives me no pleasure in typing this, but spades have to be called rectangular-shaped digging objects.

The best parts of the track are few and far between; the opening riff and the sonically submerged guitar solo (1.07 – 1.19, and again at 2.13 – 2.32) are reasonable, but nothing more than that. The 'stalker-in-waiting' themed lyrics, and low-pitched backing vocals create an unpleasant mood which comes across as just plain weird when set against the summery-sounding, poppy musical accompaniment. Confused and disjointed, and displaying a bizarre mixture of styles and ideas, 'Ricochet Man' is firmly in the running for the 'most disappointing song on the album'. But there's some stiff competition ahead …

'Back in My Arms' (4.12)

Devlin saves the day for the end of what used to be side one with this light, country-influenced mid-tempo ballad. 'Back in My Arms' benefits from a restrained arrangement; instruments come and go, adding subtly to the sound, allowing the song to grow from relatively peaceful beginnings to a more muscular conclusion. The production has a soft-focus, 'end of the 1970s' feel to it.

A tasteful guitar introduction over a simple bass, acoustic guitar, and light drum backing opens proceedings, and Devlin's vocals are front and centre in the mix. The lyrics, and his delivery of them, are both excellent: 'I recall her now, that face from a thousand magazines, in a crowded room where dancers swayed and laughter tumbled through the haze. When her eyes met mine, and all of the laughter stopped at once, and I swear she used that golden hair, and whispered words that only I could hear …'

The chorus is excellent, melodic and memorable, even when sung without the enhancement that backing vocals will add when it reappears. What helps the power of this section is the modulation from G major for the verse up into A major. This is a clever device which lifts the music temporarily before falling back into G major for the next verse. That said, this apparently simple song goes through an unusual verse chord progression (G major, F major, B minor, F sharp minor, D major, C major) before the more confident and persuasive I, IV and V basis used for the chorus.

'Back in My Arms' sounds like The Eagles when they went into ballad mode, and it's a strong indication of Devlin's melodic sensibilities, which would shine strongly on his astrology themed, 1983 solo album *Breaking Starcodes*. There, as here, there is a genuine melodic strength which makes each of the songs a minor pop masterpiece. Is it Horslips? No, of course, it isn't, at least not as we know it, Jim, but a good song is a good song and must be acknowledged.

A sustained violin tone from the keyboards is a constant throughout the second verse, with some occasional, country guitar fills. The second chorus is even better, thanks to the addition of the harmonised backing vocals, and the post-chorus guitar solo is *exactly* right for this song. Spacious, tuneful, and full of feeling, it builds in intensity over the chorus chord progression, before the song lapses back into another evocative verse: 'How times have changed and yesterday's smile seems thin today. I can't bear to see your features fall, can't take another image on the wall…'.

The coda section is dedicated to repeats of the chorus. Normally this would smack of needless repetition, but here the melody and arrangement is so strong that the music doesn't become dull. The vocals are faded out, leaving just the instrumentation playing away, with a beautiful keyboard tune, developed from the seventeenth-century harp melody 'Tab Har Dom Do Lauh', making its way through as this, too, fades away.

If *Short Stories* had seven other songs with the melodic strength and sense of purpose of 'Guests of the Nation', 'Back in Your Arms', and 'Rescue Me', 'Horslips 2.0' might have had more success. As it is, these tracks are the diamonds in the rough, and the terrain is about to get a lot harder …

'Summer's Most Wanted Girl' (3.28)

An interesting keyboard ostinato, with a funky drum and bass backing, introduce the next O'Connor composition. And sadly, once again, it's not up there with his best work. The tempo is sluggish, the band sound tired and uninspired, and lyrically it's nothing special, documenting the life of the 'end-of-season' girls at holiday resorts.

The short chorus has the best line and musical lift: 'Summer's most wanted girl became winter's loneliest fool'. The only other moment of any real interest is the too-short instrumental after the second chorus, where Devlin has that rarity – a bass solo! Normally this could be a cause for concern, but here it's better than what's gone before or comes after it. Another chorus hoves into view, and 'Summer's Most Wanted Girl' trudges off mournfully into the distance, unloved, and soon to be forgotten.

This is another track which pulls in multiple directions, and consequently fails to achieve anything apart from relief when it's finished. I don't want a Horslips album to engender these feelings, but *Short Stories* just keeps doing this to me. Next witness ...

'Amazing Offer' (3.10)

'If you tick this box, you get a money-back guarantee'. This is the opening line, sung a capella by O'Connor. I am not joking. If those words had been put on the album sleeve, it would have saved a lot of suffering amongst the fan base. And many applications for refunds. The lyrics concern a man eager for a relationship advertising himself like a household product. In the deft hands of a band like Squeeze, this could have worked. Here it sounds tired, limp, and weak.

There's a distinctive new wave feel to this mid-tempo rocker. Elvis Costello springs to mind as someone who could knock out an easily superior song before breakfast. The chorus is bubblegum-pop light tripe, and whilst there is a spirited guitar solo mid-way through, there is a strong feeling that the majority of the rest of the band are phoning in their contributions for this desperately sub-average composition.

Bereft of an engaging melody or involving lyrics, 'Amazing Offer' is neither amazing nor offers anything positive. I don't like being this sort of reviewer – I really don't – but this song and the majority of *Short Stories* just makes my teeth itch.

'Rescue Me' (3.24)

What an appropriate title. 'Rescue Me' is the first song on the album where you realise you have stumbled across a genuine *Horslips* song. The best composition on *Short Stories* by a country mile is, according to Devlin:

> ...in a completely different league and very much in the vein of 'Blackbird' (The Beatles, from *The White Album*). The melody of the chorus was written

> around the concertina tune 'The Downfall of Paris'. I wrote it to be played on guitar with a pick, but if you play it chorded it sounds Far Eastern, which was intentional because it was about the Vietnamese boat people, who were at the time undergoing a much more cruel version of the enforced emigration the Irish had undergone a century and more earlier... I later realised that, subconsciously, it was also about myself and the way I felt towards the band at that point. We were falling apart.

Light years away from O'Connor's compositions, 'Rescue Me' breathes effortless class, both lyrically and musically. It's understated, simple in structure, and played and sung with great style. Largely reliant on just a beautifully recorded acoustic guitar and a relentless, simple bass drum beat, Devlin's vocal phrasing and tone are stunning. Some gorgeous, gentle, and well-harmonised backing vocals appear for the chorus ('Pointing my way home' and 'Drift the sea alone') and the song is all the better for their sparse inclusion.

There's nothing overdone here; the production is crisp and clear, giving the music space to breathe and allowing the listener to focus on the strength of the track. Nothing gets in the way of Devlin's voice and the guitar; this is a song born of folk club open-mic nights, proof, if it were needed, that all you need to make magic is good lyrics and music, and the ability to portray both with equal effectiveness. When other instruments appear, they add to the music, both by their inclusion and subsequent absence.

But there's more. At 1.37, a counter-melody appears amongst the backing vocals. It's a concertina! Welcome back, my friend, to the show we thought had ended. And it gets better, as the instrumental features O'Connor (for it is he) and Lockhart on flute playing a harmonised duet. This section is the musical equivalent of the first fresh air after getting off a flight on a budget airline. It's the first time when you think, 'Oh, thank God, they *have* still got it'.

A further chorus featuring concertina, flute, and the backing vocals bring this minor masterpiece to a close. And that, ladies and gentlemen, is how it's done.

'The Life You Save' (3.59)

Heavy on the reverb, and the first song on the album to be sung by Lockhart, 'The Life You Save' is a ballad which suffers from 'Too Much, Too Soon' syndrome. At times it sounds like he is fighting for sonic space with the busy electric guitar, O'Doherty's (uncredited) piano, the backing vocals and an intrusive tambourine played by that well-known anagram Ztak Evets, (Steve Katz).

The chorus is the best part of the song, both musically and lyrically: 'All the love you gave won't bring him home. And the life you save could be your own' and there are some effective harmony vocals sitting back in the mix, but, overall, the sound is cluttered. The traditional tune 'Roisin Dubh' ('Black Rose') is concealed within the chorus.

What spoils what could be an otherwise perfectly serviceable track is the sonic busyness; there are hints of the problems that beset *The Man Who Built America*; there's a lot going on for a lot of the time, and there doesn't need to be. If the arrangement was stripped back and the reverb dialled down, the song would have a better chance of engaging with the listener. As it is, the 'big ballad' feel that the band seem to be striving for never really coalesces, and the inevitable fade really can't come soon enough.

'Soap Opera' (3.22)

Appropriately enough to round off the album, 'Soap Opera' is another 'relationship gone wrong' lyric. This time, O'Connor is back to front the song, which is another pacey rocker with some sideways steps into occasional pseudo-prog rock.

Again, lyrically, it's no cause for celebration: 'Suddenly she's on the phone to all her so-called friends. It looks like she's in agony, is it real or let's pretend? And just as quick she's on her knees, must be the latest trend. Her eyes wide open like a child saying please can we make amends'. On the (very limited) positive side, O'Connor's breathless vocal style suits the narrative.

Musically, 'Soap Opera' is the most complex song on *Short Stories*, (although that's not saying much), with plenty of variance in instrumentation and mood. It's more involving than the previous O'Connor's compositions, but there's only so much that can be done with such relatively poor material. Whilst it sounds like the band is doing their manful best, the whole is not greater than the sum of the parts. There's a lot going on, and the points where the music calms down from its pop-rocky bias (0.17, 0.48, 1.58, and 3.03) are where it becomes more interesting. In better times, these ideas would have been developed further and could have led to a stronger final track.

But inspiration, it seems, has left the building, especially with the last verse; 'Now she's in the bathroom, what the hell is going on? I'm shouting, 'Take it easy baby, I know there's something wrong" – oh dear. The chorus is no better: 'I love her, I love her, I love her, I love her, I wish the girl would see. I love her too much sometimes. I can't let her make a soap opera out of me'. I am not joking, those *are* the lyrics.

Ironically the song closes on a major chord on the keyboard, which is at odds with the mournful, aggressive nature of the rest of the track. And, like its televisual namesake, 'Soap Opera' comes across as ultimately a depressing experience.

And, for a band which prided itself on mood-lifting, powerful final tracks, 'Soap Opera' is a confused and confusing end to an album which, despite hints of former glories, does little but disappoint and frustrate the listener. It's not a great epitaph to what would be viewed as a (mostly) illustrious career. I applaud the band for never wanting to repeat themselves (although I would be more than happy to have been treated to, for example, 'A Second Book of Invasions') *Short Stories,* on the whole, trashes their reputation in one fell swoop. It is telling that only one track ('Guests of the Nation') would make it onto the final album of the band's first era; the well-received *The Belfast Gigs*, which is fundamentally a 'Greatest Hits – Live' collection.

And that, as far as anyone could tell, was the end of Horslips. But like a hawk, they would swoop and swoop again. But only after what has been described as taking the longest tea break in rock and roll history. Do hawks take tea breaks? These do…

Roll Back (2004)

Personnel:
Eamon Carr: drums, percussion
Barry Devlin: bass, vocals
Johnny Fean: guitar, tenor guitar, slide guitar, tenor banjo, vocals
Jim Lockhart: piano, keyboard, low whistle, vocals
Charles O'Connor: guitar, tenor guitar, violin, concertina, mandolin, vocals
Recorded at Grouse Lodge Studios, Horsleap, County Westmeath
Produced by Horslips
Engineered by Stefano Soffia and Ivan O'Shea
Mixed by Stefano Soffia
Mastered at Abbey Road Studios by Peter May
All tracks composed/arranged by Carr, Devlin, Fean, O'Connor, and Lockhart
Released on 3 December 2004
Issued on Horslips Records (MOO23)

Following the release of *Short Stories*, Horslips toured North America again, playing a lot of the new album's material alongside established crowd favourites. Into 1980, and the band toured Ireland twice, including three nights at the Whitla Hall, Queens University, Belfast. Two of these performances were recorded by Steve Katz, using the Manor Mobile, with a determination to produce a better live representation of the band than had been achieved with *Horslips Live!*

On 18 July, *The Belfast Gigs* was released, together with a single taken from it: 'Shakin' All Over' (a heavyweight cover of the 1960 hit by Johnny Kidd & The Pirates) with 'Sword of Light' on the B-side. Lockhart's view of what he believed would be the band's swansong was:

> As a live album, I thought it did a great job of preserving a moment in time. There were reels and reels of multi-track tapes from *The Belfast Gigs* that didn't get used. We were planning to issue two volumes of that album, probably a year apart, but by the time we would have looked at putting together the second volume, the tapes had disappeared from our office.
>
> I thought those recordings were really well done and I take my hat off to Steve Katz, who organised the mobile side of things so smoothly. The results were definitely a huge improvement over the roughness of the previous *Horslips Live*.

Producer Katz said:

> It was effectively a farewell party. They were ready to unleash all their frustrations on stage and have a great time, and I think that really comes over on the record. They really nailed that one.

He's right: *The Belfast Gigs* is the sound of a band playing their hearts out to a wildly enthusiastic audience. The tracklisting is a high-energy parade through past glories:

'Trouble (With a Capital T)', 'The Man Who Built America', 'The Warm Sweet Breath of Love', 'The Power and the Glory ', 'Blindman', 'Shakin' All Over', 'King of the Fairies', 'Guests of the Nation', 'Dearg Doom'

The 2011 remaster edition included the previously 'single-only' release: a spirited version of 'Sword of Light' as a bonus track. In keeping with the excitement captured by Katz, the cover continued the theme. O'Connor, of course, takes up the story:

> For *The Belfast Gigs*, Susan Byrne was employed to photograph the band on stage at the Whitla Hall, with the emphasis on action rather than nice, well-composed portraits. She was right up there with us, and because she was a girl, we allowed her closer access than a bloke! It was Sue's first proper gig shoot, and that can be scary in such a boisterous environment. Perhaps her inexperience showed in the grainy, sometimes slightly blurred results, but that was precisely the flavour we were looking for. We knew that we wanted this live album to capture the intensity of our performance, so we went all out to make the package enhance that feeling, right down to the stencil font that mimicked our flight cases. Billy Moore worked to my brief on the final art, and what makes it for me is the audience at the front looking up at the band and the unbridled excitement of it all comes flooding back.

Touring across Ireland continued throughout the summer and early autumn, and, on 8 October 1980, at the Ulster Hall in Belfast, Horslips played the final show of the first stage of their history. There was no big row, no inter-band fights; they just all agreed to part company. Devlin observed:

> We had known for three or four months that we would be going our separate ways and didn't tell anybody. Nothing was announced about Ulster Hall being our last show and there was never any suggestion that we would bow out with a big farewell tour. The band congregated backstage afterwards, shook hands and said, 'See you in the next life', only it was a lot more emotional than that.

A very brief summary of what the individual members did during the intervening decades prior to their 21st-century reformation was given to RTÉ by Lockhart in March 2022:

> The lads (I can say that?) busied themselves on other and varied fronts: drummer Eamon Carr is a journalist, sports pundit, and art aficionado; bassist

Barry Devlin writes for film and TV and graphic novels; multi-instrumentalist Charles O'Connor (already an art aficionado) became a dealer in antiques and musical instruments, and Johnny Fean continued to hone his guitar hero skills to even greater heights. And I worked until recently in RTÉ Radio, mostly with Dave Fanning. But everyone also kept a finger in some musical pie or other…

During their absence as a band, Horslips was the subject of two compilation albums: *The Horslips Collection* was released on 29 March 1981 on the K-Tel label with a tracklisting of:

'King of the Fairies', 'Flower Amang Them All', 'Johnny's Wedding', 'Daybreak', 'Furniture', 'Loneliness', 'King of Morning, Queen of Day', 'Dearg Doom', 'Trouble (With a Capital T)', 'The Man Who Built America', 'I'll Be Waiting', 'The Power and the Glory', 'Speed the Plough', 'Long Weekend', 'Guests of the Nation'

A more comprehensive compilation, *The Best of Horslips*, emerged on 7 May 2002 on the Edsel/Demon label, containing:

'Hall of Mirrors', 'Furniture', 'Faster Than the Hound', 'Dearg Doom', 'More Than You Can Chew', 'Time to Kill!', 'Nighttown Boy', 'Mad Pat', 'Blindman', 'The Blind Can't Lead the Blind', 'The Snakes Farewell to the Emerald Isle', 'Flirting in the Shadows', 'Everything Will Be Alright', 'Trouble (With a Capital T)', 'Sideways to the Sun', 'Sword of Light', 'Warm Sweet Breath of Love', 'The Power and the Glory', 'Speed the Plough', 'Come Summer', 'Stowaway', 'Ghosts', 'Loneliness', 'I'll Be Waiting', 'The Man Who Built America', 'Long Weekend', 'Rescue Me', 'Summer's Most Wanted Girl', 'Guests of the Nation'

In April 2000, having reclaimed the rights to their entire catalogue after a fifteen-year-long legal battle with the Belfast-based Outlet Recording Company, all the original albums were remastered with engineer Peter Mew at Abbey Road Studios, London. Over the next five years, the twelve original albums would all be reissued.

In the spring of 2001, Lockhart, Fean, Devlin and O'Connor assembled at O'Connor's home in Whitby, West Yorkshire, with the tentative idea of writing some new material together. Carr was unable to attend due to other commitments. Approximately 40 minutes worth of material was recorded, but the project was eventually abandoned. However, the seeds of what would become *Roll Back* were sown, as Lockhart remembered:

We worked up some nice ideas with some sample loops, dug out some untested traditional tunes, and also revisited a few oldies from a different angle. One of these rehashes proved to be the foundation for the *Roll Back* version of 'Trouble (With a Capital T)', which came out of the blue when Johnny picked up his guitar and started to play a bottleneck slide riff.

On 24 March 2004, the band reunited to give their first live performance together in nearly a quarter of a century. This was at the opening of the exhibition 'History of Horslips' at the Orchard Gallery in Derry, organised by three uber-fans (Jim Nelis, Paul Callaghan, and Stephen Ferris). It ran for two weeks, and then went 'on tour' around Ireland, proving to be the blue touchpaper that launched Horslips as a performing band once more.

Roll Back was recorded during the summer of 2004 and released on 3 December, together with a limited edition bonus disc, 'Music From an Exhibition', which included the four live, acoustic-based tracks the band had played in Derry: 'Flower Amang Them All', 'Furniture', 'The Musical Priest/The High Reel', and 'Trouble (With a Capital T')', together with video clips from the Orchard Gallery. The mini boxset included a sixteen-page booklet featuring the song lyrics and the following text:

> When we were writing these songs all those years ago, they were full of different possibilities, other ways to go. We made choices then that resulted in the arrangements that appeared on twelve albums and countless gigs. Recently we thought it might be a good idea to explore other, quieter lives for some of those songs, to take them back to their starting points and go the road we might have taken back then.

The booklet included five individual photos of the band. None of them are smiling, but they should be because *Roll Back* is a joy to listen to from beginning to end. Familiar songs are rearranged and given the 'unplugged' treatment, which allows new sonic light to shine through old windows. It is fascinating to listen to these new interpretations played in an almost entirely acoustic setting, and to compare and contrast with the originals. It proves the adage that a good song works in any number of arrangements and reinterpretations, and *Roll Back* gives us fifteen prime examples of this. The recording is crisp and superbly balanced between the instruments to the extent that it feels like the band are in the same room as the listener, playing just to them. Whilst there are, sadly, no new songs, we are treated to three solo instrumentals: 'Huish the Cat', 'Ace and Deuce', and 'My Love is in America'.

The songs which undergo the most illuminating transformation are the rockers: 'The Man Who Built America', 'The Wrath of the Rain', and 'Blindman' are completely reworked, reinterpreted, and delivered with a freshness and spirit which is inspirational. The ballads are inevitably closer to the originals in feel, if not instrumentation. 'Flirting in the Shadows' and 'Long Weekend' come out extremely well as a result of their makeovers.

Horslips did, of course, have more than enough material to chew over to issue a second album of reinterpretations. Time, circumstance, and, of course, their long-held belief that they should never tread musical water may have prevented them from releasing a sequel, but just imagine hearing 'Charolais', 'Everything Will Be Alright', or 'King of Morning, Queen of Day' in a new, acoustic setting. This strikes me as a missed opportunity.

Fryer, the producer of *Dancehall Sweethearts* and *The Unfortunate Cup of Tea!,* had this to say about the very welcome new/old album:

> I always thought Horslips had more left in them. *Roll Back* is the sound of five people having the time of their lives, the five people I remember. I love how they rearranged some of those old numbers and injected so much love, creativity, and enthusiasm, into them. It's much more mature and it comes over as a superbly entertaining album…which is what Horslips were always about.

'Trouble (With A Capital T)' (3.53)

Dispensing with the high-powered flute and guitar introduction of the original in favour of a new piano and acoustic guitar opening, *'Roll Back'* immediately sets out its credentials. The tempo is slower; the feel is relaxed, less urgent and, whilst the song structure (verse, chorus, etc.) is the same, the acoustic rearrangement puts this classic number into entirely different sonic territory.

The slide guitar sounds excellent, the bass and drum ground the song with subtlety, and O'Connor's vocals, given more space thanks to the slower tempo, are evocative and expressive. Lockhart provides some gentle Fender Rhodes keyboard backing and the degree of reverb added to the sound really lifts it into a laid-back, bluesy mood. There is some neat, rhythmic tambourine for the final verse and chorus, and Fean has some very tasty lines in the coda section. The track comes to a close with a sustained tambourine fading away over the keyboard chords.

'The Man Who Built America' (3.46)

The major alteration from the barnstorming original is the change of time signature from a stomping 4/4 to a lilting 6/8. Gone are the strident organ introduction and the backing vocals. This interpretation is fundamentally just vocals, a strummed acoustic guitar, subtle bass, and some highly effective drum patterns in the background. The tempo is again slower, giving Fean more time to get inside the lyrics, and Lockhart imitates the absent harmony vocals with piano phrases in the chorus. The overall effect of these changes is 'less is more', and it's stunning.

Another unusual departure occurs after the second chorus when there is a highly melodic violin solo section (2.04 – 2.35) in place of the anticipated guitar contribution. O'Connor makes a further appearance after the final chorus, playing over a slow fade.

'Guests of the Nation' (3.39)

The best rock song on *Short Stories* goes all Delta-Blues. Again, the time signature shifts, this time from 4/4 to 2/4, the tempo is slower, and there is a steady, laid-back groove at work throughout the track.

'Guests of the Nation' opens with two acoustic guitars playing a melodic introduction a world away from the foot-stamping urgency of the original. Devlin's first line ('There's too much rain for drive-in movies...') has the bass and drums joining in on 'drive-in'. I like the idea that the band suddenly realised that they should have been playing at this point and just pile in. The arrangement is too clever for such mischief, of course, but it's an interesting flick of the musical wrist. It would have been far easier to let the song runs its first verse with just vocals and guitars and then bring in the rhythm section. Neat.

Some tasteful slide guitar in the lead-up to the chorus brings in the excellent harmony vocals, and there is also a simple slide solo after the second chorus. The post solo chorus adds some banjo (an instrument not heard since *Drive the Cold Winter Away*) before a melodic coda brings this excellent reinterpretation to an end.

'Faster Than the Hound' (4.13)

The mandolin is missing from the new arrangement, and the long-sustained organ chords, which were a constant thread through the original are now replaced with phrases on the electric piano. The dominant instrument throughout is a gently plucked acoustic guitar. There are no backing vocals, and the original's distorted guitar solo is replaced with a more introspective organ instrumental section.

The climactic lines ('I travelled Ireland in a day...') are still powerful, but remain restrained and controlled, supported by some celebratory-sounding organ chords at the back of the mix. The net effect is that *Roll Back*'s 'Faster Than the Hound' sounds more like an alternative take from *The Táin* sessions rather than a new interpretation. This version is slightly quicker (76 beats per minute as opposed to 66 on the original), but never feels rushed or inappropriate.

'Huish the Cat' (2.30)

A jig played by O'Connor on the acoustic guitar, 'Huish the Cat' is captivating. Recorded in a single take, with the guitar in an open G major tuning with some slide playing and just the right amount of reverberation to add depth to the sound, this is a beautiful performance of a traditional Irish tune.

'Mad Pat' (4.09)

The dynamic variation of the original is dispensed with here. This 'Pat' is just O'Connor on vocals, and a steady arpeggio-based acoustic guitar accompaniment. After the first chorus, there is a short, very pretty violin solo, with some counterpoint lines appearing during the second verse and chorus. The instrumental section (2.26 – 2.52) remains just violin and guitar, with the final chorus leading to a beautiful coda section where, out of the blue, a pair of harmonised flutes play long sustained notes behind the violin and guitar, the music slowing to a gentle halt.

The differences between this simple, highly affecting version and the original are startling. Like two sides of the same coin, it is impossible to say which is better, that is just determined by your mood at the time – and possibly age!

'The Wrath of the Rain' (2.49)
The jaunty 4/4 time shuffle makes a surprisingly effective transition into 3/4 (waltz) time with Devlin and a twelve-string guitar holding court over the first verse. A concertina appears for the tail end of the chorus, a relaxed bass and drum backing join for the second verse, with the concertina adding much to the sound throughout.

Fean adds in a soaring slide solo (1.33 – 1.53) and he continues to contribute throughout the third verse and chorus, along with the concertina, the track coming to an end on the word 'alone' after a reprise of the first line of the lyrics. The music sustains on a C major chord, leaving a sense of anticipation rather than the anticipated closure with a tonic G major.

'Flirting in the Shadows' (3.37)
I much prefer this version to that on *The Unfortunate Cup of Tea!* This is also the first track on the album where the natural sound of the acoustic guitar has been treated with a deep, slow, flanged modulation effect. This creates a suitably unsettling atmosphere, whilst O'Connor's close-mic vocals are also highly effective.

There is plenty going on in this arrangement, comparatively, which strengthens this reinterpretation. The instrumental has mandolin and acoustic guitar trading lines, with some slide guitar appearing at the end of the bridge section. The bass pulses away throughout the song, linked to some understated drumming. 'Flirting in the Shadows', in this incarnation, comes across as an involving and atmospheric number.

The only 'off' moment, and it seems churlish to mention it, occurs right at the end of the track. After the repeated line 'tugging at my sleeve', there is a sudden, rushed downward slide effect on the guitar; it sounds unnecessary and clumsy, spoiling the last few seconds of the track.

'Cú Chulainn's Lament' (3.50)
Acoustic guitar and a quiet bodhran presage Devlin's crystal clear vocal of one of the best songs on *The Táin*. The chorus lifts magnificently with a combination of gorgeous harmony vocals, and a stunning cello part courtesy of guest musician, Aisling Drury Byrne. This really adds depth to the arrangement, and Byrne continues to play melodic phrases for the second verse and the instrumental at 1.28. Here, slide guitar takes centre stage with a simple, elegant solo, and then the fantastic bridge section is reprised.

The play-out instrumental (2.45 onwards) has Lockhart's low whistle playing a wistful solo, complimented by the ever-present acoustic guitar and cello in the background. This is truly excellent stuff, and a really good rearrangement of a ballad which offers a fascinating alternative to what we are used to hearing. Hats off to whoever thought of including a cello here, and, of course, to Byrne for her mesmerising performance.

'Ace and Deuce' (2.04)
'Ace and Deuce' is a piper's practice tune last heard on *Happy to Meet....* For this album, it is played solely by Fean on a tenor guitar, a four-string instrument tuned in the same fourth intervals as a violin. He gives the traditional tune a spirited performance, the recording highlighting the intricacies of the techniques needed to bring the music to life.

'Blindman' (2.45)
Like its sister song 'Mad Pat', the 'Blindman' of *Roll Back* is stripped right back to its basics. Opening with acoustic guitar and O'Connor's vocals, it builds gradually with the addition of bass and soft-sounding bodhran for the second section; 'Don't you ever feel like dancing when the evening turns to gold?' This combination, with an extra layer of highly effective guitar, continues through the second verse, until a ghostly-sounding mandolin and slide guitar instrumental section (1.37 – 2.14). Here Fean and O'Connor trade melodic lines back and forth before their tones merge for the final bars. The third verse is just guitar and vocals and the song ends, like 'The Wrath of the Rain', hanging in the air without a definitive ending...

'Furniture' (3.21)
The epic ballad from *Happy to Meet...* becomes something smaller and more intimate whilst still maintaining its inherent power in a quieter context. 'Furniture' opens with strummed acoustic guitars, understated vocals, and electric piano for the first verse and chorus. Backing vocals appear in the chorus to great effect, with bass and drums providing a lift for the second verse. Lockhart's paean to his supportive parents gains extra emotional heft in this rendition, with the passing of time.

Byrne's cello is added to the second chorus, which adds still more controlled power to the track. In place of the original's big central riff ('Oro Se Do Bheatha Bhaile'), which formed the basis of the extended instrumental section, we have a short guitar and mandolin duet. This leads into a reprise of the chorus, the song coming to a gentle crescendo, closing with the final words 'Out of the archer's view' and a sustained chord.

'The Power and the Glory' (3.12)
One of the defining songs on *The Book of Invasions*, 'The Power and the Glory', like the other rocking racks on this collection, undergoes a substantial instrumental rewrite.

Played on the acoustic guitar rather than a keyboard, the first two notes of the original's anthemic introduction remain, but the rest of the melody is altered and set against an almost 'muzak' backing, emphasised by the syncopated claves which are heard in the verse. The pace is slower than before, backing vocals join for the chorus, together with some lovely nylon-strung guitar playing, and there is a dramatically phrased violin solo after the second chorus.

This is followed by further choruses and a changed ending; the repeated 'We're gonna take it, we're gonna take it' line from the original is replaced by a short instrumental coda.

'Long Weekend' (4.08)

This interpretation sounds like an alternate take for *The Man Who Built America* sessions which was subsequently rejected. Based initially around just vocals and acoustic guitar, long, sustained keyboard chords gradually appear during the second verse, becoming more prominent as the song progresses. Backing vocals enhance at various key points ('Shout she cries', 'Phone she pleads', 'Write she says', and 'Comeback some time') together with short slide guitar phrases. The instrumental section (2.30 – 3.28) is a hypnotic blend of guitar, sustained keyboards and cymbal washes.

Unlike the *The Man Who Built America* recording, this version has less reverb, making the performance more personal and confessional. This makes it, to my ears, superior to the original, ending with another hanging-in-the-air chord, waiting for resolution: 'On the corner she is sitting, expecting him to *show…*'. The low sustained keyboards continue and a solitary bell-tree chimes to finish the song.

'My Love is in America' (2.59)

A reel played by O'Connor on the tenor guitar, this is a missed opportunity for an 'all band' instrumental along the lines of 'Sorry to Part' from the debut album. 'My Love is in America' is an up-tempo piece which gets the feet tapping, with some displays of impressive technique showcased by the appearance of slide and palm muting. But how good would it have been to hear some coughing, a pint glass chinking, or maybe someone saying 'Time, gentlemen, please…' before everyone joins in?

Such an arrangement would have been a fabulous 'doff of the cap' to the band's past, and, if *Roll Back* lacks anything, it is a track which celebrates the skill of the five musicians playing purely as instrumentalists. We could have been treated to modern-day acoustic-based replays of 'The High Reel', or 'The Silver Spear'. As it is, *Roll Back*, whilst not exactly petering out, doesn't end with the sense of reinvention and celebration which is prevalent across the rest of the album.

More Than You Can Chew (2023)

The three years that followed the return of Horslips, which had begun with a small exhibition and gathered steam with a full-blown new album, saw them appearing on The Late Show on RTÉ, 'Other Voices' in Dingle, and an 'Ardan Horslips Special' concert at RTÉ Studios for TG4. These were all private gigs in studio settings, and thoughts turned to the bigger question: is there still a live audience out there to play too? In the interim, fans were treated to the first ever full-length documentary on the band when *The Return of the Dancehall Sweethearts*, written and directed by Maurice Linnane, was released in 2005.

In the summer of 2009, serious rehearsing took place, resulting in two major shows: one at the Odyssey in Dublin, and the other at the O2 in Belfast. Carr didn't feel he could give enough of himself to be involved in the performances, and instead suggested Ray Fean, Johnny's younger brother and a well-respected drummer. The two concerts were triumphant successes. The O2 gig was recorded and released, with the imaginative title of *Live at the O2*, on 19 November 2010. A new DVD, *The Road to the O2* (subtitled 'A Film About Getting To The Gig') appeared simultaneously. The tracklisting for the CDs was:

'King of the Fairies', 'The Power and the Glory', 'Mad Pat', 'Blindman', 'The Wrath of the Rain', 'Furniture', 'The High Reel', 'Faster Than the Hound', 'The Piper in the Meadow Straying', 'Long Weekend', 'Rescue Me', 'Maeve's Court', 'Charolais', 'Daybreak', 'Drive the Cold Winter Away', 'Ride to Hell', 'Sideways to the Sun', 'Sword of Light', 'Flirting in the Shadows', 'Ghosts', 'Speed the Plough', 'Sure the Boy Was Green', 'I'll Be Waiting', 'The Man Who Built America', 'Trouble (With a Capital T)', 'Dearg Doom', 'Loneliness', 'Warm Sweet Breath of Love'

2011 saw the band perform at the Waterfront Hall, Belfast, with the 69-piece Ulster Orchestra, whose parts had been arranged and were conducted by Brian Byrne. The concert was broadcast live on BBC Radio Ulster, with fans listening online worldwide. In Ray Fean's absence, the drum seat was filled by Paul McAteer. On 25 November, the concert was released as a new live CD: *Live With The Ulster Orchestra* with a tracklisting of:

'Daybreak', 'The Power and the Glory', 'Fantasia (My Lagan Love')', 'Drive the Cold Winter Away', 'Ride to Hell', 'Sideways to the Sun', 'Dusk', 'Sword of Light', 'Setanta', 'Maeve's Court', 'Charolais', 'More Than You Can Chew', 'March Into Trouble', 'Trouble (With a Capital T)', 'Dearg Doom', 'Rescue Me', 'Ghosts', 'King of the Fairies', 'I'll Be Waiting'

On 1 November 2013, *Biography*, a new 23-track two-disc compilation CD focussing purely on the band's singles, was released. The first CD featured

'A'-sides:
'The High Reel', 'Dearg Doom', 'More Than You Can Chew', 'Nighttown Boy', 'King of the Fairies', '(If That's What You Want) That's What You Get', 'Warm Sweet Breath of Love', 'The Power and the Glory', 'Speed the Plough', 'Loneliness'

The second CD collected together the respective B-sides:

'Furniture', 'The Shamrock Shore', 'Faster Than the Hound', 'We Bring the Summer With Us', 'Sunburst', 'The Snakes' Farewell to the Emerald Isle', 'King of Morning, Queen of Day', 'Sir Festus Burke', 'Bridge From Heart to Heart', 'Red River Rock (Live)', 'Long Weekend', 'Homesick'

The two previously unreleased tracks were aural catnip for fans:

'Bridge From Heart to Heart' (2.50)
This song and 'Red River Rock (Live)' were on the B-side of the single 'Speed the Plough' released on 23 June 1978. An outtake from the recording sessions for *Aliens*, 'Bridge From Heart to Heart' features plenty of Lizzy-esque harmony guitars in a solid pop-rock number sung by Fean. Two brisk verses later, and there's a half-tempo section (0.29 – 0.41) leading to another verse. The instrumental section (0.55 – 1.38) passes to the flute. At 1.25, the tempo reverts to half-speed and the secondary melody from 'Exiles' ('the 'Carrickfergus' section) makes an unexpected appearance.

There is then a return back to full tempo with more verses (including the excellent lyric 'The nights are long without you here, the days go by like heavy weather'), and plenty of flute counterpoint. A further half-time section blends the vocal melody with the 'Carrickfergus' excerpt again, then it's quickly back into full tempo for the coda section with a final chorus, some neat three-crotchet beat rest sections, and the song coming to a tight end.

'Bridge From Heart to Heart' is a fascinating insight into the band circa *Aliens*. Whilst it is an enjoyable slice of pop-rockery, there is no doubt that the better tracks made it to the album.

'Red River Rock (Live)' (1.49)
Along with 'Shakin' All Over', 'Red River Rock' is the only non-band composition to appear on a Horslips record. Written by King, Mack, and Mendelsohn, and originally a hit for Johnny & The Hurricanes in July 1959, Lockhart leads the band with his organ set to extra cheese as befits the track.

Taken at a furious tempo, Fean unleashes a brutal and typically early rock'n'roll style solo (0.50 – 1.03). The energy goes up a further notch with a key change from C to D major, the music ending with a clumsy cut off which loses the fans' obvious approval.

Originally intended to celebrate the 50th anniversary of the release of *Happy To Meet...*, and finally unleashed in February 2023, *More Than You Can Chew*, is a 35(!) disc retrospective. Initially and accurately titled *The EnormoBox*, it contains over 350 audio tracks, sixteen hours of unreleased material, and nearly five hours of unreleased video footage.

So, what do you get for the, let's be honest, considerable financial outlay? Well, the packaging is first-class, bordering on luxurious. The high-quality black box opens smoothly to reveal a weighty, high-quality hardback book *On The Record* written by Mark Cunningham, and a thinner, yet still comprehensive paperback *Lyricography*, also compiled and edited by Cunningham. Some reproduction newsletters from the 'Horslips Funky Fan Club', a poster for the band's gig at the National Stadium, Dublin on Saturday, October 14 1972, featuring the 'egghead imagery', and five individually signed photos of the band taken by Ian Finlay in 1976 for *The Book Of Invasions* rear sleeve complete the package. The main event is, of course, the discs themselves, all presented in mini cardboard sleeves.

First out of the box, we have all the original albums the band issued between 1972 and 1980, 'newly mastered'. Erm, okay. But any serious fan will already have these, and, 'newly mastered' or not, the decision to include them is less than impressive. The inclusion of *Roll Back* and one of the subsequent live albums only serves to underline this. There is an anomaly here; *Live at the O2* is included, and yet *Live with the Ulster Orchestra* is not. But the box set is supposed to be the 'complete' output of the band. Yes, yes, I know, there are plenty more discs to enjoy, but first impressions and so forth ...

This gripe aside, do the 2022 versions sound any better than the series issued ten years ago (which included some 'bonus' live tracks which now appear as part of this collection), or the band-authenticated CD reissues from the turn of the decade after the long legal battle which secured the band's ownership of their work? Well, the differences, such as they are, are subtle. The sound is a fraction crisper and the definition and separation between the instruments is very slightly improved, but this is marginal. It may be possible to get more than an aural cigarette paper between the differing discs, but such a task is better suited to an audiophile with tens of thousands of pounds worth of hi-fi equipment, and I'm not one of those people.

All in all, however, this is a highly impressive, quality-laden, 'pride of place' purchase, worth both the weight and the wait. There's a lot of listening and watching here, so to avoid needless repetition, I have only offered commentary where a track is 'new', or where there are marked differences from the familiar version.

Disc 14: Tracks From The Vaults (Volume 2)

'Ace & Deuce' (3.06), 'More Than You Can Chew' ('45 single remix) (3.10), 'Nighttown Boy' ('45 single edit) (3.12), '(If That's What You Want) That's What

You'll Get' ('45 single edit) (4.57), 'The Power And The Glory' ('45 single remix) (4.02), 'Sir Festus Burke' (B-side) (2.18)

'Ace & Deuce' (3.06)
This is a very pretty rearrangement with a six-string and a twelve-string guitar and a mandolin playing this charming instrumental.

'Horslips presents Horslips: An advance look into *The Man Who Built America* (13.14)
'Bridge From Heart To Heart' (2.51), 'Red River Rock' (1.48), 'Welcome To Céilí House' (7.53), 'When Night Comes' (3.02), 'Back in my Arms' (Alternative Mix) (4.33), 'Unapproved Road' (Alternative Mix) (3.43), 'Guests of the Nation' (Alternative Mix) (3.21), 'Sword of Light' (Live) (5.49), 'Sure The Boy Was Green' (Live - Previously Unreleased) (4.44), 'Sandymount Strand/Shilly Shaddle' (2.31), 'One Final Ace & Deuce' (2.41)

A very amusing pseudo interview-cum-documentary from members of the band interspersed with excerpts from 'Loneliness', 'The Man Who Built America', 'Homesick', 'Green Star Liner', 'Tonight (You're With Me)', and 'I'll Be Waiting'.

'Welcome To Céilí House' (7.53)
This is another entertaining eight minutes of mucking about in the studio taking the mick in spectacular fashion out of a typical Irish radio traditional music show, and themselves. This finally comes to a chaotic end, only to be replaced by a truly horrendous version of 'San Francisco', the 1967 song written by John Phillips of The Mamas & the Papas, and sung by Scott McKenzie. This then morphs into a mock rock'n'roll number. It's as daft as it is fun to listen to, and this is the sound of the band letting their hair down after another day's recording.

'When Night Comes' (3.02)
A Fean composition which was the B-side to the single 'Guests Of The Nation', 'When Night Comes' is an up-tempo power pop song which has more going for it than quite a few of the tracks on *'Short Stories…'*. Whilst it's good enough for that album it's nowhere strong enough to make it onto any of the bands' preceding records. Fean's guitar soloing is suitably aggressively melodic, and the chorus is catchy with some good backing vocals and sprightly piano playing, but overall this song is no hidden gem.

'Back in my Arms' (Alternative Mix) (4.33)
The sublime backing vocals, and Fean's exceptional guitar solo are absent.

'Unapproved Road' (Alternative Mix) (3.43), 'Guests of the Nation' (Alternative Mix) (3.21)

'Sword of Light' (Live) (5.49)
This is preceded by 'Dusk', as is the case with most of the versions of the song included in the box set.

'Sure The Boy Was Green' (Live - Previously Unreleased) (4.44)
'Sandymount Strand/Shilly Shaddle' (2.31)
A previously unissued recording from the *'Roll Back'* sessions, this is a pair of up-tempo mandolin pieces played with exceptional dexterity by O'Connor, and again a wonderful recorded sound.

'One Final Ace & Deuce' (2.41)
This is first track of this CD again, but this time with an added reflective soliloquy spoken by Devlin. His words include references to 'furniture', 'the power and the glory', and 'ghosts', in an entirely fitting, poignant final track.

Disc 15: Live 1973 - '75
Dublin Stadium; 28 May 1973:
'Happy To Meet' (1.46), 'Hall Of Mirrors' (8.26), 'Scalloway Ripoff' (3.30) 'Dance To Yer Daddy' (4.34), 'The Musical Priest' (6.19)

Some of the debut's album's tracks are given a live airing, with 'Scalloway Ripoff' and 'The Musical Priest' being particularly impressive.

Dancehall Sweethearts Rehearsals
'The Sweets Of May' (0.49), 'Sunburst' (0.56), 'Mad Pat' (2.42), 'The Blind Can't Lead The Blind' (0.35), 'Nothing To Say (A Lifetime To Pay)' (2.12)

'The Sweets Of May' (0.49)
This is a short, mid-tempo solo mandolin piece.

'Sunburst' (0.56)
This is a purely instrumental extract, showcasing an intriguing 'work-in-progress', featuring just piano, bass and guitar.

'Mad Pat' (2.42)
An interesting rearrangement with Lockhart's piano to the fore of the mix alongside the familiar mandolin. The five bars leading into the chorus are different to the recorded version. Again, a 'song-in-development' *sans* drums

'The Blind Can't Lead The Blind' (0.35)
A very funky bass and drum rhythm with a slinky electric guitar riff on top offer up an intriguing 'what might have been' version of the track.

'Nothing To Say (A Lifetime To Pay)' (2.12)
Devlin's vocals are supported solely by acoustic guitar, piano, and flute in this fascinating early recording of what would be the final track on *Aliens*. Despite the absence of bass and drums, this demo still rocks along, with Lockhart being especially busy on the flute.

My Father's Place, New York, 1974:
'More Than You Can Chew' (3.50), 'Dearg Doom' (3.51), 'Lonely Hearts' (6.04) 'Furniture' (10.41), 'The High Reel' (2.39)

The band play spirited versions of songs from *The Tain* and *Danceball Sweethearts*, with 'Dearg Doom', and 'The High Reel' being the standout performances.

The National Stadium, Dublin: 1975:
'Everything Will Be Alright'/'Rakish Paddy' (3.59), 'You Can't Fool The Beast' (4.42), 'More Than You Can Chew' (3.00), 'Dearg Doom' (3.39)

The three *Táin* songs are played as a medley, with the crowd particularly loving 'Dearg Doom', which strangely fades midway through a chorus.

'Everything Will Be Alright'/'Rakish Paddy' (3.59)
Introduced by an announcer talking over the band who are midway through the song, he manages to get out of the way in time for the first instrumental section, the final verse and chorus, and the segue from 'The Trip To Durrow' into 'Rakish Paddy'.

Disc 16: Live In Berlin 1976
'Hall of Mirrors' (4.57), 'Daybreak' (2.55), 'Drive the Cold Winter Away' (1.06), 'Ride to Hell' (3.50), 'Sideways to the Sun' (4.44), 'Sword of Light' (6.20), 'The Rights of Man' (3.54), 'Dark' (2.29), 'Furniture' (12.44), 'Charolais' (3.53), 'More Than You Can Chew' (3.12), 'Silver Spear' (2.42), 'King of the Fairies' (4.17), 'Dearg Doom' (4.53), 'The High Reel' (2.49), 'Rakish Paddy'/'Johnny's Wedding' (5.23)

'The Rights of Man' (3.54)
This is a cracking little instrumental, reinterpreting a beautiful traditional hornpipe, with a skilful arrangment which gives the individual instruments plenty of space to shine. Opening with some delicate guitar work, the flute has the first tune. Drums and bass add energy to the guitar backing, and the melody is passed to the electric mandolin. A second tune appears before the music builds to a rousing rock guitar solo (1.49 – 2.10). This is reprised on the mandolin; then some savage power chords summon in the quiet

introduction. The mandolin continues the original tune, with the second melody swiftly following again. A repeat of the power chords leads into a big finish, a roll of drums, and a direct segue into 'Dark'.

The thought occurs; where could this have sat on *The Book of Invasions*? 'The Rights of Man' is an excellent example of the fusion approach that Horslips pioneered, and would have been worthy of greater exposure.

'Dark' (2.29), 'Furniture' (12.44), 'Charolais' (3.53), 'More Than You Can Chew' (3.12), 'Silver Spear' (2.42), 'King of the Fairies' (4.17), 'Dearg Doom' (4.53), 'The High Reel' (2.49)

'Rakish Paddy'/'Johnny's Wedding' (5.23)
This is a rare live version of the single which set the band's career in motion.

Disc 17: 'Live 1977'
Boston:
'New York Wakes' (4.02), 'The Wrath of the Rain' (2.59), 'Sideways to the Sun' (4.10), 'Dearg Doom' (7.05), 'Bim Istigh Ag' Ol' (5.58)

London:
'New York Wakes' (4.00), 'The Power and The Glory' (3.38), 'The Rocks Remain' (3.07), 'Mad Pat' (6.38), 'Blindman' (3.18), 'Daybreak' (3.44), 'Drive the Cold Winter Away' (1.48), 'Ride to Hell' (3.09), 'Sideways to the Sun' (3.47), 'Sword of Light' (6.13), 'Dark' (0.53), 'Sure The Boy was Green' (4.33), 'Warm Sweet Breath of Love' (4.01), 'Trouble (with a Capital T)' (3.23)

Disc 18: Rehearsals 1976–'77: The Book of Invasions & Aliens
'Aililú Na Gamhna' (1.55), 'Trouble (With A Capital T)' (3.11), 'Kilfenora (King of Morning)' (3.58), 'Fantasia (My Lagan Love)' (2.40), 'Trouble (with a Capital T)' (1.08), 'Mother of Pearl (The Rocks Remain)' (2.46), 'Johnny's Riff (The Power And The Glory)' (1.10), 'Trouble (with A Capital T)' (3.14), 'The Power And The Glory' (1.48), 'Warm Sweet Breath of Love' (3.07), 'The Power and The Glory' (2.48), 'Come Summer' (Version 1) (1.26), 'Seán Ó Dí' (1.27), 'Mother Of Pearl (Duo)' (1.37), 'Aililú na Gamhna' (4.01), 'Come Summer (Version 2)' (1.36), 'Highway' (Version 1) (1.49), 'Highway' (Version 2) (3.25), 'Crossroads / Fead An Iolair' (1.48), 'Little Man' (0.40), 'Come Summer (Version 3)' (1.43), 'Second Avenue (Harmonies)' (0.36), 'Second Avenue' (3.48), 'Come Summer (Harmonies)' (0.37), 'Sure The Boy was Green (Harmonies)' (1.50), 'A Lifetime To Pay' (3.50), 'Stowaway' (3.05), 'Mailman' (1.35), 'Páistín Fionn (Fair-Haired Child)' (1.28), 'Come Summer' (Version 4) (2.14), 'A Dancer after Dreams' (2.12), 'The Wrath of The Rain' (2.48), 'Aililú na Gamhna / Highway' (3.18)

'Aililú Na Gamhna' (1.55)
This is a mid-tempo instrumental featuring organ, bass, and drums with an overlaid electric mandolin.

'Trouble (With A Capital T)' (3.11)
A brisk rendition with some indistinct, ad-libbed vocals and a different melody. This version lacks the finished song's half-tempo instrumental section.

'Kilfenora (King of Morning)' (3.58)
The instrumentation and arrangement is all pretty much in place here. Only the vocals are at an experimental stage, being more markers than a finalised version. There is an inventive guitar solo, together with some busy flute playing.

'Fantasia (My Lagan Love)' (2.40)
Whilst this is a rehearsal room play through, featuring guitar, bass, drums and flute, it is very close to what ended up on the album.

'Trouble (with a Capital T)' (1.08)
This is the first verse of the song with just a guide electric guitar and two-part harmonised vocals

'Mother of Pearl (The Rocks Remain)' (2.46)
Instrumentally familiar, this early version of 'The Rocks Remain' has some 'first draft' lyrics, the vocal melody already being established.

'Johnny's Riff (The Power And The Glory)' (1.10)
This is Fean playing the 'behind the keyboard tune' chord sequence against a syncopated bass and drum rhythm, with Lockhart playing the organ melody..

'Trouble (with A Capital T)' (3.14)
Another instrumentally secure version with the vocals are still under some degree of consideration.

'The Power And The Glory' (1.48)
The chorus guitar riff is featured here with bass and drums, and some keyboard harmonies.

'Warm Sweet Breath of Love' (3.07)
A rousing rendition helped by the inclusion of some tasty slide guitar fills, which put a different slant on the arrangement.

'The Power and The Glory' (2.48)
An instrumental-only version of the track, this recording has a different chord and melody structure to the second half of the first and second verses ('You can see the dawn-a-coming…the daybreak's here', and 'Not so much teachers as fighters … ring 'em right'). This track finishes at the end of the second chorus.

'Come Summer' (Version 1) (1.26)
A short, instrumental-only version, with flute, bass, guitar, and syncopated drums.

'Seán Ó Dí' (1.27)
Played on the organ with bass joining for the reprises, this attractive tune regrettably never saw the light of day in a Horslips song.

'Mother Of Pearl (Duo)' (1.37)
A duet featuring acoustic guitar and flute, with Devlin singing the 'needs more work' lyrics.

'Aililú na Gamhna' (4.01)
Introduced by Lockhart over the nicely funky bass riff ('Welcome to Ballyvaughan. Sun, sea, sand … and cross-rhythms!'), this is an instrumental, driven by Carr's drums with the electric guitar and keyboards taking turns with the main melody. There's a very real sense that this could have been developed into something very impressive.

'Come Summer (Version 2)' (1.36)
This is very close to the album version, with only the vocals missing. It consists of just the introduction, a verse, chorus, finishing with a repeat of the introduction.

'Highway' (Version 1) (1.49)
A 'work-in-progress' recording of what would eventually become 'Green Star Liner', with ad-libbed words and vocal melody line.

'Highway' (Version 2) (3.25)
This takes the great, mid-paced groove from 'Aililú na Gamhna' and adds Devlin's vocals, and mandolin to make a song which could have easily held its own on both *Aliens* and *The Man Who Built America.*

'Crossroads / Fead An Iolair' (1.48)
Featuring just piano and Devlin's singing, this music would become the backbone of 'Green Star Liner'.

'Little Man' (0.40)
A nylon strung guitar and vocal melody which would later appear as 'Come Summer', the excellent lyrics ('You know you've got to hustle when you live out on the street, can't find a shelter when there's deadlines to meet, and your friends don't want to know you so you've turned on the heat, Little Man') being discarded and sadly never reused.

'Come Summer (Version 3)' (1.43)
Another 'virtually album' version, this track benefits from the addition of O'Connor's mandolin. Again, it consists of just the introduction, a verse, chorus, fading after a repeat of the introduction.

'Second Avenue (Harmonies)' (0.36)
Guitar and bass are the only instrumental backing to the vocal harmonies for the chorus of the song,

'Second Avenue' (3.48)
An 'all guns blazing' take of the complete song, the only omission being the transition from 4/4 to 6/8 time at the end, which heralded in 'The Morrison's Jig'.

'Come Summer (Harmonies)' (0.37)
The electric guitar is the only instrumental backing to the vocal harmonies for the chorus of the song.

'Sure The Boy was Green (Harmonies)' (1.50)
Bass and guitar provide the accompaniment for the intricate layers of voices for the songs' verses and choruses.

'A Lifetime To Pay' (3.50)
A raw version, with Lockhart surely suffering from lip blisters by the end of the session. Fean's guitar lines sometimes tipping the cap towards The Beatles, and Devlin is very busy on the bass during the coda of this energetic track.

'Stowaway' (3.05)
Another 'very close to the familiar' rendition, except for the inclusion of O'Connors' fiddle playing. The vocals are so far back in the mix as to be virtually inaudible.

'Mailman' (1.35)
This begins as a guitar and flute duet before being joined by bass and finally, drums. It's a melodic and effective chord progression which could have been the basis of a 'country' flavoured song. O'Connor's violin is heard distantly in the background, providing some counterpoint harmony lines.

'Páistín Fionn (Fair-Haired Child)' (1.28)
Flute and acoustic guitar play a duet version of this charming tune which sounds like it has escaped from the *Drive The Cold Winter Away* sessions.

'Come Summer' (Version 4) (2.14)
Another instrumental version of the song featuring guitar, flute, mandolin, bass, and drums. This is very close to the definitive track.

'A Dancer after Dreams' (2.12)
The song that became 'Ghosts' on *Aliens*, 'A Dancer after Dreams' features Devlin instead of Fean on vocals. There are some minor variations here to the recorded versions' lyrics and arrangement, and the track finishes after two verses.

'The Wrath of The Rain' (2.48)
This has a distinctly country rock feel to it, whilst maintaining the shuffle rhythm of the album version. Fean's guitar dominates, whilst the interesting contributions from Lockhart and O'Connor are less discernable.

'Aililú na Gamhna / Highway' (3.18)
A slower yet still funky feel pervades the sinuous groove of this intriguing 'one that got away'. Devlin's vocals are not forward enough in the mix to fully realise the song's potential. Instrumentally, however, it's a great listen.

Disc 19: Live 1978 - '79 (Disc 1)
Sigma Sound Studios, Philadelphia. March 23 1979:
'The Power and The Glory' (4.30), 'Blindman' (3.22), 'The Man Who Built America' (4.23), 'Homesick' (4.39), 'Tonight (You're With Me)' (3.51), 'Blitzkreig Bop' (2.56)

'Blitzkreig Bop' (2.56)
After an amusing introduction implying that the audience are about to hear from the band's acoustic roots, The Ramones song gets a high energy thrashing from Horslips with split backing vocals and the electric mandolin adding a fresh slant to this classic punk song by the four 'brothers'. Strangely, this fades away without capturing the audiences possibly stunned reaction. The recording quality of the Sigma Sound recording is excellent throughout.

Ulster Hall, Belfast. November 14 1978:
'Second Avenue' (3.45), 'New York Wakes' (3.58), 'Speed the Plough' (3.21), 'Loneliness' (4.12), 'King of the Fairies' (4.58), 'Dearg Doom' (6.31)

Rehearsals. Glencolmcille, County Donegal. July 7 and 8, 1978
'The Man Who Built America' (2.03)
'The Man Who Built America' (2.03), 'Jam' (0.28), 'If It Takes All Night' (1.47), 'Law On The Run' (1.21), 'It'll Be Alright (Summer Comes Along)' (2.36), 'Long Weekend (Instrumental)' (1.08), 'Letters From Home' (3.00), 'I'll Be Waiting' (5.57), 'Long Time Ago (Harmonies)' (3.15), 'Long Time Ago' (3.54), 'Long Weekend (Instrumental)' (3.26)

A rough and ready recording where guitars and drums largely dominate the other instruments, except for the occasional loud keyboard flourish. The track finishes after the second chorus.

'Jam' (0.28)
This is a very short, aggressive guitar, keyboard, bass, and drums sequence that doesn't really do anything, go anywhere, or stay in the memory.

'If It Takes All Night' (1.47)
This is a truncated version of the track with plenty of the familiar arrangements in place. It comes to a close after the second chorus.

'Law On The Run' (1.21)
A short, slower, bluesy version with the vocals being virtually indiscernable.

'It'll Be Alright (Summer Comes Along)' (2.36)
A poppy rocker driven along by Carr's drumming, the song would later be recorded by Devlin for his solo album *Breaking Starcodes* as 'When Summer Comes Around'. It was the non-album B-side of the single 'Who Can Tame The Lion?'

'Long Weekend (Instrumental)' (1.08)
Guitars, bass, and drums create an evocative mood in this short section from the beginning of the song.

'Letters From Home' (3.00)
This opens with some intricate three-part harmony singing of the song title before the band join in with a slower-tempo version of the song. The vocal harmonies also stand out in the choruses.

'I'll Be Waiting' (5.57)
This is the band stretching out in a full-length play-through. Nearly all the details of the album version are in place, and Fean goes to town on his long, intense solo.

'Long Time Ago (Harmonies)' (3.15)
This is another 'ready for the studio' version with all the integral musical elements in place. The vocal harmonies are a further strong feature.

'Long Time Ago' (3.54)
Commencing with organ and guitar playing the chorus refrain, the vocal harmonies on 'All I know is it was a long time ago' are again impressive, with the band joining for another run-through of the song.

'Long Weekend (Instrumental)' (3.26)
Another track showcasing Fean's superb tone and expressive phrasing over a moody backing.

Disc 20: Live 1978 - '79 (Disc 2)

The Bottom Line, New York. April 6 1979:

'The Man Who Built America' (4.36), 'New York Wakes' (3.46), 'Homesick' (3.56), 'Culture Clash (When Irish Eyes Are Smiling)' (1.27), 'Wrath Of The Rain' (2.50), 'Daybreak' (4.07), 'Drive The Cold Winter Away' (1.28), 'Ride To Hell' (3.16), 'Sideways to the Sun' (3.55), 'Sword Of Light' (5.38), 'Dark' (1.43), 'Speed The Plough' (3.16), 'Sure The Boy Was Green' (4.41)

'Culture Clash (When Irish Eyes Are Smiling)' (1.27)
This is an unexpected reggae-rock instrumental version of the traditional tune, with organ and distorted guitar sharing the tune, which segues into 'Wrath Of The Rain' (2.50).

The Spectrum, Philadelphia. March 24 1979

'Daybreak' (4.07), 'Drive The Cold Winter Away' (1.28), 'Ride To Hell' (3.16), 'Sideways to the Sun' (3.55), 'Sword Of Light' (5.38), 'Dark' (1.43), 'Speed The Plough' (3.16), 'Sure The Boy Was Green' (4.41)

There is a clumsy instrumental link into 'Dusk'. The mix of the recording of 'Speed The Plough' is unbalanced, which highlights O'Connor's intricate mandolin playing within the arrangement.

My Father's Place, Roslyn, New York. March 28 1979:

'Silver Spear' (2.29)

An Irish Ballroom. 1979:

'If It Takes All Night' (3.28), 'Loneliness' (4.14), 'Tonight (You're With Me)' (3.34)

Rather Ripped Records, Berkeley, California. May 17 1979:

'The High Reel' (2.51), 'King Of The Fairies' (4.19), 'Shakin' All Over' (4.19), 'I Saw Her Standing There' (2.02), 'The Hucklebuck' (2.25)

'I Saw Her Standing There' (2.02)
Whilst 'Shakin' All Over' was a staple in the bands' live set list, their true musical heroes were The Beatles. This is a rare recording of Horslips paying enthusiastic homage, with Devlin on vocals.

'The Hucklebuck' (2.25)
Another rarity, this dance-craze starter originally recorded by Paul Williams and His Hucklebuckers in 1949, is a perfect example of the band having a lot of fun on stage. The lead vocals are taken by Horslips' crew member Paul Verner. Sadly it fades, so we don't hear the entire song, but the playing is tight and the energy is tangible.

Disc 21: The Last Gig: Ulster Hall, Belfast, 8th October 1980
'Guests Of The Nation' (3.38), 'Unapproved Road' (3.08), 'Warm Sweet Breath Of Love' (3.47), 'Speed The Plough' (3.05), 'Sure The Boy Was Green' (4.58), 'Summer's Most Wanted Girl' (3.49), 'Soap Opera' (3.41), 'Trouble (With A Capital T)' (3.37), 'Loneliness' (4.21), 'King Of The Fairies' (4.57), 'The Power and The Glory' (3.37), 'Blindman' (3.32), 'The Man Who Built America' (4.03), 'Amazing Offer' (3.13), 'Ricochet' (3.35), 'Shakin' All Over' (5.46), 'Dearg Doom' (6.40)

The songs from *'Short Stories...'* are not as well received by the crowd as the 'classic' tracks.

Disc 22: The Last Gig (Encores) Live 1980, 2004 & 2011 Live
'Sword Of Light' (8.25), 'The Last Time' (3.34)

'The Last Time' (3.34)
The final song of the final gig, and it's a high energy, punkish blast through the classic 1965 Jagger/Richards composition.

Irish Ballroom; 1980:
'When Night Comes' (3.11)

Charlestown; May 1980:
'Law On The Run' (2.49)

Irish Ballroom; 1980:
'The Wrath Of The Rain' (2.52), 'I'll Be Waiting' (8.01)

Whitla Hall, Belfast; 1 May 1980:
'Motorway Madness' (3.35)

'RTÉ, 2012: Horslips Recall The Final Gig' (7.08)
Miriam O'Callaghan discusses the Ulster Hall gig with all five band members in a good-humoured and amusing interview.

Derry Exhibition; May 2004:
'Flower Amang Them All' (3.15), 'Furniture'/'The Musical Priest'/'The High Reel' (7.50), 'Mad Pat' (4.35), 'Trouble (With a Capital T)' (6.19)

This is the all-acoustic version of the band with the songs played live at the small-scale exhibition, which set the ball rolling a second time.

Ulster Hall, Belfast. 23 September 2011:
'Sword Of Light' (6.16), 'Mad Pat' (6.57)Discs 23, 24, and 25 are the *Roll Back* and *Live At The O2* CDs, respectively.

Disc 26: In Session At RTÉ 1971

'Flower Amang Them All' (2.27), 'Bonny at Morn' (2.13), 'Ace & Deuce' (4.22), 'Carolan's Frolic' (1.44), 'Passing Through' (5.50), 'An Bratach Ban' (1.54), 'Lay The Bent to the Bonny Brook' (5.18), 'Buttered Peas (Take 1)' (1.27), 'The Snow It Melts the Soonest (Take 1)' (1.01), 'Traps' (2.00), 'The Tern and The Swallow' (3.25), 'Buttered Peas (Take 2)' (1.32), 'The Snow It Melts The Soonest (Take 2)' (3.42)

'Bonny at Morn' (2.13)
A charming concertina, banjo and bodhran accompaniment backs O'Connor's delicate vocal treatment of this traditional eighteenth-century Northumbrian tune.

'Passing Through' (5.50)
This is a cover of the song by the English rock group Steamhammer, first released on their 1969 album *Mk II*. Opening with a syncopated bass, tasteful, clean electric guitar from Declan Sinnott, and some gentle percussion, a central melody on the concertina is then joined by the flute in counterpoint. Sinnott takes the lead vocals, and the overall sound is very much 'of its time'. 'Passing Through' is a track built for improvisation, with contributions from flute and violin being prominent, and a 'fuzz' guitar solo (3.37 – 4.36), which illustrates Sinnot's abilities. Another verse and chorus and further improvisation lead the song to a close.

'Lay The Bent to the Bonny Brook' (5.18)
A gentle ballad which builds with bell-like keyboards, acoustic guitar, bass, and bodhran is a showcase for Lockhart's vocal performance. A textbook example of 'less being more' as the arrangement and dynamics ebb and flow.

'Buttered Peas (Take 1)' (1.27)
This is a mid-tempo, very catchy, whistle, concertina and bodhran instrumental.

'The Snow It Melts the Soonest (Take 1)' (1.01)
Concertina, acoustic guitar and flute play a pensive version of the tune, which comes to an abrupt halt during the first verse.

'Traps' (2.00)
A Sinnot/Carr composition, 'Traps' is a ballad for acoustic guitar and vocal. Sung by Sinnot, Carr's talents as a lyricist are illustrated with some evocative lines, including 'Behind the black November trees, gulls and rooks swirl cock-a-hoop, weave their tragic memories' and 'Silver glimmers in your hand, thorns in your eyes'.

'The Tern and The Swallow' (3.25)
This is a beautiful ballad sung by Devlin backed by an acoustic guitar and concertina.

'The Snow It Melts The Soonest (Take 2)' (3.42)
This is a complete take of the song at the slower pace with some uncertainties in the melodic and chordal accompaniment.

Larry Lynch Recordings, 1971:

'Courtesan' (4.41)
'Courtesan' (4.41), 'Johnny's Wedding' (3.26), 'The Clergy's Lamentation' (5.07)

Another Sinnott/Carr composition, 'Courtesan' is a blend of electric and acoustic guitar, bass, flute, and cymbal washes which combines to create a moody texture. This changes abruptly at 1.03 with an increased tempo and the appearance of Sinnott's understated vocals.

Pulsing percussion, harmony vocals, mandolin, and flute all add to the change of style, which takes time signature alterations in its stride. 'Courtesan' is an intriguing peek behind the curtain as to what might have been had Sinnott stayed with the band; the music is introspective and intriguing, the opening returning to act as a coda section.

'Johnny's Wedding' (3.26)
Distorted guitar dominates the opening to this high-energy piece, with bass and drums both busy in the background. Thirty seconds in, and the tune is handed over to O'Connor on the mandolin. There's a busy interplay between mandolin and guitar throughout the track, sometimes playing in unison, then alternating between melody and chordal accompaniment. A menacing section of fuzz guitar begins at 1.56 before a brief, lighter mood, which builds to a frenetic conclusion with a tight, syncopated ending.

'The Clergy's Lamentation' (5.07)
Sinnott's contributions in the introduction (natural harmonic bends with the tremolo arm, some bluesy runs) are another fascinating insight into a possible future. The familiar tune begins at 1.12 and the roadmap to *Happy To Meet…* is clearly now well established…

Disc 27: 'In Session At RTÉ 1972'

'Green Gravel' (1.13), 'Charles O'Connor: Interview' (4.22), 'Knockeen-Free (Maeve's Court)' (1.59), 'Jim Lockhart Interview' (4.34), 'Fairy King / Blody'r Drain' (3.54), 'Eamon Carr Interview' (5.43), 'The Clergy's Lamentation' (5.24), 'Barry Devlin Interview (Part One)' (3.06), 'An Bratach Bán' (2.59), 'Barry Devlin Interview (Part Two)' (3.17), 'Scalloway Ripoff' (3.27), 'Comb Your Hair And Curl It' (4.53), 'Passing Through' (5.39), 'Furniture' (8.13), 'An Bratach Bán' (3.00), 'Johnny's Gone To France' (2.58), 'Scalloway Ripoff' (3.27)

The first eleven tracks are taken from an RTE broadcast, *All The Wild Sweetness* broadcast on 8 October 1972. The remainder were recorded at 'Kens Klub, also broadcast in September 1972.

'Green Gravel' (1.13)
This is a short version which only manages to get through two verses before it fades away.

'Charles O'Connor: Interview' (4.22)
All five interview tracks were recorded in September 1972, in the gap between the departure of Gus Guest and the arrival of Johnny Fean. All the interviews feature the band member just talking about themselves, the band, and the music; there is no interviewer.

'An Bratach Bán' (2.59)
There is a different mid-section tune from that presented on *'Happy To Meet…'* with some spectacular fiddle playing (1.57 – 2.59)

The final six tracks are from a radio programme titled 'Ken's Klub, from September 1972, which was hosted by Ken Stewart.

'Comb Your Hair And Curl It' (4.53)
The vocals are absent, the section being dominated instead by the electric guitar and drums before building through a furious crescendo into a powerful close.

'Passing Through' (5.39)
This is an unnecessary second inclusion of this cover version, this time featuring Devlin on vocals.

'An Bratach Bán' (3.00)
Another virtual retread of what we have just heard, with the same 'new' tune in the second half.

'Johnny's Gone To France' (2.58)
A traditional melody that really should have made it onto the debut album, 'Johnny's Gone To France' is a fine piece of mid-tempo duetting between whistle and fiddle for the main theme, driven along by guitar, bass and drums. At 1.09 a key change summons in a new tune with a drone mandolin and bass accompaniment which builds with the full rhythm section kicking in at 2.05. This track is a genuine hidden gem, fresh, energetic, extremely well played and arranged; it fits right in with the band's unique musical direction.

Disc 28: 'The RTÉ Sessions 2003 – 2012'
This CD is the sound of the band in re-arranged, acoustic *'Roll Back'* mode.

Mystery Train: 16 February 2005:
'The Man Who Built America' (3.38), 'Furniture' (3.14), 'Huish The Cat' (1.57), 'Mad Pat' (3.37), 'Trouble (With a Capital T)' (3.41), 'Dearg Doom' (2.18)

'Dearg Doom' (2.18)
This was one of the surprise omissions from *'Roll Back'*. Acoustic guitars and O'Connor's vocals dominate initially, with some occasional percussion. Fean has an excellent but too-brief mid-song solo.

Miriam Meets...:15 August 2009
'Flower Amang Them All' (2.07), 'Dearg Doom' (3.50), 'Trouble (With a Capital T)' (3.51), 'Furniture' (6.18)

The latter three tracks all benefit from the full rock band treatment with exceptional clarity, tone, and energy.

John Murray Show: 29 October 2010:
'Green Star Liner' (2.16), 'Trouble (With a Capital T)' (2.06)

'Green Star Liner' (2.16)
Another very welcome re-imagining of one of the band's less well-known songs, 'Green Star Liner' gets the acoustic treatment shining new light by featuring just Devlin's vocals, an acoustic guitar, flute and bodhran.

'Trouble (With A Capital T)' (2.06)
This is the *Roll Back* arrangement.

Today With Pat Kenny: 12 December 2012:
'The Snow That Melts The Soonest' (2.57), 'Sword of Light' (3.23)

The Snow That Melts The Soonest' (2.57)
This is a beautiful new interpretation whilst still retaining its acoustic roots. It is taken at a slightly faster tempo than the original. The addition of percussion adds much to this new arrangement.

Gerry Ryan, Live, RTE: 6 April 2005:
'The Man Who Built America' (3.29), 'Furniture' (3.00), 'Dearg Doom' (2.23), 'Trouble (With a Capital T)' (3.28)

These four tracks are the *Roll Back* reinterpretations.

'Horslips Story with Eamon Carr, Jim Lockhart, and Barry Devlin' (15.55)
Excerpts from the album versions of 'Furniture', Faster Than The Hound', 'Time To Kill', and 'Dearg Doom' punctuate this potted history of the band from its inception up to 1980.

Disc 29: The Host: Tryal (1984) & Singles

'Witness Stand' (2.40), 'First Kiss' (3.15), 'Vows and Breezes' (5.01), 'Safe World' (3.23), 'Declaring War' (5.06), 'Walk on Love' (3.49), 'Unearthly Hours' (3.49). Shadowy Figures' (3.10), 'I Wanted You' (3.16), 'Strange Disease' (3.29), 'Dark Light and Air (Break a Spell)' (2.55) 'The Long Walk' (4.11)

Carr, Fean, and O'Connor reunite (with the addition of Chris Page on bass and Peter Keenan on keyboards) to revisit the idea of the concept album; the subject this time being the burning of the alleged witch, Bridget Cleary, in Tipperary in 1895. A lack of any traditional instrumentation, and an over-reliance on the production techniques of the period spoil an otherwise intriguing project.

Disc 30: Fean & Carr: Live and Studio 1984 – 86

'Maud Gonne' (03.07), 'Turn Back, My Love' (04.07), 'At The Hawk's Well' (03.05), 'Overture' (00.47), 'A Flame Forever Burning' (03.58), 'The Hellhound Was My Name' (04.29), 'Home Sweet Broken Home' (02.57), 'Coconut Grove' (02.45), 'Still I'm Sad' (02.51), 'Chasing Dragons' (03.02), 'William and the Lady' (04.42), 'Kitty's Rambles' (02.23), 'The Hidden Curriculum' (02.24), 'Dolly's (The Hidden Curriculum Outtake)' (02.05), 'The Hellhound Was My Name' (03.25), 'The Trip, The King & The Creel' (03:01), 'Circular Riff Jam' (05.50), 'The Road To Lisdoonvarna' (01.51), 'Don't Give Up On Yourself' (04.42), 'Pipeline / Johnny's Tune' (04.30), 'Maud Gonne' (03.16)

This features a mixture of tracks by Carr and Fean collaborating together with a variety of other musicians, and more from The Host, this time without O'Connor. There's a mixture of acoustic and electric numbers, some instrumentals, and a handful of raw, live tracks. Some Celtic elements appear in this wide-ranging collection of both originals and cover versions. The standout track is, without doubt, 'The Hellhound Was My Name', which is a rousing, aggressive single by The Host, represented here in both studio and live version.

Disc 31: Breaking Star Codes: Barry Devlin

'Twins (Gemini)' (03.38), 'Who Can Tame the Lion? (Leo)' (03.30), 'It's the Cruellest Sign (Virgo)' (03.23), 'Remember You're a Winner (Aries)' (03.53), 'When Two Stars Collide (Sagittarius)' (04.15), 'Just Another Line (Pisces)' (03.02), 'Let the Scales Decide (Libra)' (03.38), 'December 21 (Capricorn)' (03.21), 'The Stars Said (Taurus)' (03.37), 'Remember a Star (Cancer)' (02.55), 'Aquarian Girls (Aquarius)' (03.37), 'Love with a Sting in its Tail (Scorpio)' (02.46), 'When Summer Comes Around' (02.19)

A gorgeous 13-track collection of highly melodic, shimmering pop-rock, with each song based around one of the twelve signs of the Zodiac. The last track ('When Summer Comes Around') was not featured on the original vinyl. Kudos also goes to Roger Dean for his impressive cover artwork and logos.

Disc 32: Uncollected Works: Jim Lockhart'

'Cré na Cille (Graveyard Clay)' (08.49), 'Errors & Omissions – End Credits' (03.09), 'Errors & Omissions – Pastoral' (01.53), 'Glenroe' (03.02), 'Gods and Gallants' (01.52), 'Great Book of Ireland – Immanence' (01.36), 'Great Book of Ireland – Main Theme' (02.28), 'Great Book of Ireland – The Dancing Pen' (01.09), 'Interlude – Achill's Hill' (0.59), 'Interlude – Fife for Fifty' (0.25), 'Interlude – Saltee Air' (0.43), 'Interlude – Shaskin Way' (0.41), 'Interlude – The Coolin' (0.42), 'Intro – Clooncunny' (0.45), 'Love Stories from Ireland' (02.04), 'Lovers of the Lake – Main Theme' (01.07), 'Lovers of the Lake – Penance Past' (01.26), 'She Moved Through the Fair (Portastudio Demo)' (03.49), 'Spring Cleaning' (02.10), 'Sunday Sport' (0.58), 'The Rime of the Ancient Mariner' (01.05), 'Thuas ag Gort a' Charnáin (Above at Gortnacarnaun)' (02.55)

Twenty-two tracks of largely instrumental music which Lockhart has composed and/or arranged for radio, television, and film over the years. Inevitably keyboard-heavy, there are some lovely touches of traditional music and instrumentation to be heard as well.

Disc 33: Angel On The Mantelpiece: The Resolution Suite; Charles O'Connor

'Ocean of Storms' (0.16), 'Seachange' (0.09), 'Comes a Calm' (0.13), 'Bottom Buttons' (0.16), 'In Your Own Time' (0.14), 'Skinner's Treat' (0.12), 'Circles Round the Moon' (0.11), 'Angel on the Mantelpiece' (0.20), 'Basket of Bones' (02.38), 'Chocolate Cats' (03.35), 'The Grand Tour' (03.05), 'When the Long Trek's Over' (02.15), 'Fiddlehead' (01.52), 'Ocean of Storms' (01.34)

This solo album is a 14-track collection of pretty instrumentals which play to all of O'Connor's compositional and musical gifts in this ode to the north-east coastal town of Whitby. The tracks are loosely based on the town's people, the folklore of the area, and the voyages of Captain Cook, who lived in the town as a child.

Disc 34: The RTE Vault: 1973 – 1979 DVD

This disc consists of videos of the band performing in Dublin and Cork between May 1973 and November 1979. There is a surprise inclusion of a cover of the Steppenwolf song 'It's Never Too Late' among the early, incendiary performances of the bands' original songs.

The eight songs from Cork promoting *Short Stories…*, from which four songs are taken, shows the fault lines that have opened up in the band by this time. Also featured is a section of song clips and conversation filmed in November 1978 at Advison Studios during the recording sessions for *The Man Who Built America*.

The Music Makers: Horslips at The Stadium 28/5/73
'Furniture', 'Johnny's Wedding', 'It's Never Too Late', 'Bi´m Istigh Ag O´l'

On Stage at The Stadium, Part One, 13/12/75
'Everything Will Be Alright', 'Rakish Paddy', 'King of The Fairies', 'Ny Kirree Fo Naghtey', 'The Piper in the Meadow Straying', 'Silver Spear, 'You Can't Fool the Beast', 'More Than You Can Chew', 'Dearg Doom'

On Stage at The Stadium, Part Two, 21/6/76
'Mad Pat', 'Blindman', 'Furniture', 'Bi´m Istigh Ag O´l', 'Johnny's Wedding'

John Molloy's Dublin, 16/7/76
'The Snakes' Farewell to the Emerald Isle', 'King of The Fairies', 'The Unfortunate Cup of Tea'

Live at Cork Opera House, 8/11/79
'Trouble (With a Capital T)', 'Amazing Offer', 'Ricochet Man', 'Summer's Most Wanted Girl', 'The Man Who Built America', 'Guest of the Nation', 'Loneliness', 'Shakin' All Over'

P.M. Documentary, 9/11/78
Song clips and talk (in Irish) filmed during The Man Who Built America's sessions at Advision Studios, London

Disc 35: 2004 – 2019 DVD

The 'Reunion Era' DVD showcases performances from 2004, 2005, 2006, 2011, 2012, 2013 and 2019. Any accusations of 'old men playing old songs to old people' are quickly put to the sword (of light) as the reformed band play with passion and precision. Also included is a 'Classic Album' documentary focussing on *Happy To Meet…*, much of which is in Gaelic.

Music from an Exhibition, 20/3/04
'Flower Amang Them All', 'Furniture', 'The Musical Priest / The High Reel', 'Trouble (With a Capital T)'

Late Late Show, 21/1/05
'The Man Who Built America'

Other Voices, 15/2/06
'The Man Who Built America', 'Furniture', 'Rescue Me', 'Trouble (With a Capital T)', 'Dearg Doom', 'Shakin' All Over'

Ardán, 25/3/06
'Trouble (With a Capital T)', 'Mad Pat', 'Ghosts', 'Furniture', 'Interview / I'll Be Waiting', 'Flower Amang Them All', 'Dearg Doom', 'Shakin' All Over'

Miriam Meets...15/8/09
'Trouble (With a Capital T)', 'Furniture', 'Dearg Doom', 'Flower Amang Them All'

Live at Cropredy Festival, 13/8/11
'Trouble (With a Capital T)'

Tall Tales Book Launch Party, 29/10/13
'The Snakes' Farewell to the Emerald Isle'

Fleadh TV, 17/8/19
'Speed the Plough', 'Sword of Light', 'Dearg Doom', 'Sideways to the Sun', 'Trouble (With a Capital T)'

1980 Belfast Gigs outtake: 2022 Montage Promo
'Sure the Boy was Green'

2004 Roll Back outtake: 2022 Promo Film
'One Final Ace & Deuce (2004 Roll Back outtake)'

Spin Documentary, 24/4/11: 2022 Promo Film
A 'Classic Albums' documentary on Happy To Meet, Sorry To Part

Sorry to Part

The success of Horslips, and their huge influence on rock music coming out of Ireland ever since, can be attributed to two main factors; their unique fusion of traditional Celtic melodies into a modern rock song setting, and the camaraderie and friendship between the five men.

The band, in the first ten years of its history, played over 2,000 concerts. They opened for hippies and closed for head-bangers. Their best albums fused highly melodic, powerful rock music with century's old traditional tunes, and with *The Táin*, and *The Book of Invasions*, they reminded Irish listeners how ancient myths still held a power all of their own.

For a band that has been, as Lockhart puts it on the DVD *The Road to the O2*, apart for three times as long as they were together, the devotion from their fan base is impressive. Of course, nostalgia plays a part in this, but at the root of Horslips is an ability to transform old music into new, vibrant rock songs which connect with people in a unique and special way. *And still does.*

When they started, they viewed themselves initially as a 'prog rock' band, and, given that this is literally 'rock which progresses', they certainly achieved this. It was the critics that dubbed them a 'Celtic Rock' band, a term to which they were not averse, but one that was never their original intention. In effect, they were a fusion band in the truest sense of the phrase; a group of highly talented, multi-instrumentalists who fused the old with the new to produce music that was rarely less than interesting, and sometimes utterly spectacular. Nobody else has produced music like Horslips, before or since, and that isn't a bad legacy to leave behind.

Assessing the band's legacy in 2004 on the *Dancehall Sweethearts* DVD, Devlin said:

> I regret enormously we didn't break America. No band ever starts out on the basis that they'll be a small band. That's not why you join a band. You want to be The Beatles. We wanted to be The Beatles, only bigger. It fact, it took us nine and a half years to realise we probably have reached our commercial potential. We had already done a great deal that's praiseworthy and that was interesting, and in some ways, we had pushed the bar high for ourselves … so, yes, there is enormous regret that you aren't U2, or The Beatles, or The Rolling Stones. And there's no 'Buts' there.

The final words go to Barry Devlin and Jim Lockhart, speaking at the end of their *BBC Radio Ulster* interview with Ralph Mclean, looking back on the band. They were asked what element of their history they were the proudest of. Devlin reflected upon the band's history thus;

> Bono (U2's singer) once said that 'Great bands are bands who do a specific thing', and he said, 'You guys did a real thing', and I think that's what I'm

proudest of. When you think Horslips, you think they did something that was quite different from what other bands did.

Lockhart had a different interpretation of the band's legacy:

I don't know if it's what we intended, but it did turn out that by bringing stuff that was our own and that belonged to the kids we were playing to, you know, that was specifically theirs as well, by bringing it to little dancehalls around the country and giving it back to them, we made a difference to a lot of people's lives that we didn't kind of appreciate until many years later. So, that meant an awful lot more than whether or not you were, like, number sixteen with a bullet in *Billboard*. Really. That's a good feeling.

It was immensely saddening to learn of the passing of Johnny Fean, who died on 28 April 2023 at his home in Shannon. He was 71. Described by Barry Devlin as 'the baby of the band', Horslips issued the following statement:

For well over fifty years, Johnny was our best friend, our creative collaborator, our guitar hero. Johnny wasn't only one of the greatest guitar players ever, he was also the sweetest man in rock'n'roll. His immeasurable talent won him countless supporters throughout the years. We remain his biggest fans. He devoted his life to music and we'll be forever grateful that he did.

The band wish to extend their heartfelt condolences to Johnny's wife, Maggie, brothers Ray, Donal, Shearie, sisters Gail and Corna, and all the extended Fean clan.

Johnny will be sorely missed.

Feans widow, Maggie, acknowledging that her husband died two days short of the 50th anniversary of the release of the single 'Dearg Doom' asked that fans play the song at noon on Sunday, 30 April. This fan was more than happy to take part, and I hope stereos the length and breadth of several lands followed suit, and at a riff-appropriate volume. That's a legacy to be proud of.

Appendix. An interview with Barry Devlin

Hello Barry. Thank you for taking the time to answer these questions, which will appear in the form of a mini-interview at the conclusion of my forthcoming book *Horslips – On Track*.

Q: For someone who has never heard of the band, which album would you recommend to them?

A: Probably *The Book Of Invasions*. It's a concept album, its quite eclectic, with anthems like 'The Power and The Glory', instrumental toons like 'Drive The Cold Winter Away', rock songs like 'Warm Sweet Breath Of Love' and the band's trademark melding of Irish instrumentals with rock rhythms and lyrics in 'Sword Of Light' and 'Trouble With A Capital T'. But, hey, you'll find something interesting on all of them. I think.

Q: Which song did you enjoy most playing live?

A: 'Dearg Doom', 'Trouble With A Capital T', 'Sword Of Light', 'Furniture' … all great fun to play. My fave though was 'I'll Be Waiting', largely because you could chill and enjoy the solo that the late, great Johnny Fean reinvented each night …

Q: What did it feel like walking on stage at the start of the O2 gig?

A: Scary. But in a good, Las Vegas way, as Homer Simpson would put it ….

Q: What do you consider the band's legacy to be?

A: Ah, Richard. I dunno. And how long have you got? I'd like to think we caught the spirit of a certain cusp moment in Ireland …

Q: Will there be an Enormo-Box 2?

A: Er, no. That's quite enough Horslips for now. Wretched excess (but in a good Las Vegas way …)

Q: Is there a 'song that got away' that you wished had made it onto a Horslips album?

A: On the rehearsals disc on the 'More Than You Can Chew' boxed set, there's a tune that can be heard morphing into a song. It's based around the melodic turns of a trad song called 'Aililiu Na Gamhna'. It never got full lyrics or even a name, but it almost beat 'A Lifetime To Pay' onto Aliens and maybe it should have …

Q: If you were to be a guest of Desert Island Discs what would your song choices be?

A: Gosh. Is it nine discs? Let's call it nine and off we go. Tomorrow it will be a different nine. And the day after..

1.. JS Bach: 'Wachet Auf (Sleepers Awake)'
2.. Beatles: 'Rain' (in fact, all the rest could be Beatles and I'd be happy under my palm tree. Rules is rules, though, so …)
3.. Al Green: 'Belle'
4.. Bob Dylan: 'Subterranean Homesick Blues'
5.. Joni Mitchell: 'Cary'
6.. U2: 'I Still haven't Found…'
7.. Warren Zevon: 'Tenderness On The Block'
8.. Blind Willie McTell: 'Little Delia'
9.. The Voice Squad: 'After Aughrim's Great Disaster'

Q: What's it like to be considered a 'living legend'?

A: Dunno about 'legend'. But that 'living' bit is excellent.

Q: Are there any plans for you (or any of the band) to write an autobiography?

A: Not me, for sure. My own eyes would glaze over with telling stories about myself, let alone those of the unfortunate reader. Anyway, the great Mark Cunningham has done all of us more justice than we deserve.
And you …
But thank you for asking.

Best wishes, and thank you Barry for the brilliant music.
Richard

Also available from Sonicbond

On Track series

Allman Brothers Band – Andrew Wild 978-1-78952-252-5
Tori Amos – Lisa Torem 978-1-78952-142-9
Aphex Twin – Beau Waddell 978-1-78952-267-9
Asia – Peter Braidis 978-1-78952-099-6
Badfinger – Robert Day-Webb 978-1-878952-176-4
Barclay James Harvest – Keith and Monica Domone 978-1-78952-067-5
Beck – Arthur Lizie 978-1-78952-258-7
The Beatles – Andrew Wild 978-1-78952-009-5
The Beatles Solo 1969-1980 – Andrew Wild 978-1-78952-030-9
Blue Oyster Cult – Jacob Holm-Lupo 978-1-78952-007-1
Blur – Matt Bishop 978-178952-164-1
Marc Bolan and T.Rex – Peter Gallagher 978-1-78952-124-5
Kate Bush – Bill Thomas 978-1-78952-097-2
Camel – Hamish Kuzminski 978-1-78952-040-8
Captain Beefheart – Opher Goodwin 978-1-78952-235-8
Caravan – Andy Boot 978-1-78952-127-6
Cardiacs – Eric Benac 978-1-78952-131-3
Nick Cave and The Bad Seeds – Dominic Sanderson 978-1-78952-240-2
Eric Clapton Solo – Andrew Wild 978-1-78952-141-2
The Clash – Nick Assirati 978-1-78952-077-4
Elvis Costello and The Attractions – Georg Purvis 978-1-78952-129-0
Crosby, Stills and Nash – Andrew Wild 978-1-78952-039-2
Creedence Clearwater Revival – Tony Thompson 978-178952-237-2
The Damned – Morgan Brown 978-1-78952-136-8
Deep Purple and Rainbow 1968-79 – Steve Pilkington 978-1-78952-002-6
Dire Straits – Andrew Wild 978-1-78952-044-6
The Doors – Tony Thompson 978-1-78952-137-5
Dream Theater – Jordan Blum 978-1-78952-050-7
Eagles – John Van der Kiste 978-1-78952-260-0
Earth, Wind and Fire – Bud Wilkins 978-1-78952-272-3
Electric Light Orchestra – Barry Delve 978-1-78952-152-8
Emerson Lake and Palmer – Mike Goode 978-1-78952-000-2
Fairport Convention – Kevan Furbank 978-1-78952-051-4
Peter Gabriel – Graeme Scarfe 978-1-78952-138-2
Genesis – Stuart MacFarlane 978-1-78952-005-7
Gentle Giant – Gary Steel 978-1-78952-058-3
Gong – Kevan Furbank 978-1-78952-082-8
Green Day – William E. Spevack 978-1-78952-261-7
Hall and Oates – Ian Abrahams 978-1-78952-167-2
Hawkwind – Duncan Harris 978-1-78952-052-1
Peter Hammill – Richard Rees Jones 978-1-78952-163-4
Roy Harper – Opher Goodwin 978-1-78952-130-6

Jimi Hendrix – Emma Stott 978-1-78952-175-7
The Hollies – Andrew Darlington 978-1-78952-159-7
Horslips – Richard James 978-1-78952-263-1
The Human League and The Sheffield Scene – Andrew Darlington 978-1-78952-186-3
The Incredible String Band – Tim Moon 978-1-78952-107-8
Iron Maiden – Steve Pilkington 978-1-78952-061-3
Joe Jackson – Richard James 978-1-78952-189-4
Jefferson Airplane – Richard Butterworth 978-1-78952-143-6
Jethro Tull – Jordan Blum 978-1-78952-016-3
Elton John in the 1970s – Peter Kearns 978-1-78952-034-7
Billy Joel – Lisa Torem 978-1-78952-183-2
Judas Priest – John Tucker 978-1-78952-018-7
Kansas – Kevin Cummings 978-1-78952-057-6
The Kinks – Martin Hutchinson 978-1-78952-172-6
Korn – Matt Karpe 978-1-78952-153-5
Led Zeppelin – Steve Pilkington 978-1-78952-151-1
Level 42 – Matt Philips 978-1-78952-102-3
Little Feat – Georg Purvis - 978-1-78952-168-9
Aimee Mann – Jez Rowden 978-1-78952-036-1
Joni Mitchell – Peter Kearns 978-1-78952-081-1
The Moody Blues – Geoffrey Feakes 978-1-78952-042-2
Motorhead – Duncan Harris 978-1-78952-173-3
Nektar – Scott Meze – 978-1-78952-257-0
New Order – Dennis Remmer – 978-1-78952-249-5
Nightwish – Simon McMurdo – 978-1-78952-270-9
Laura Nyro – Philip Ward 978-1-78952-182-5
Mike Oldfield – Ryan Yard 978-1-78952-060-6
Opeth – Jordan Blum 978-1-78-952-166-5
Pearl Jam – Ben L. Connor 978-1-78952-188-7
Tom Petty – Richard James 978-1-78952-128-3
Pink Floyd – Richard Butterworth 978-1-78952-242-6
The Police – Pete Braidis 978-1-78952-158-0
Porcupine Tree – Nick Holmes 978-1-78952-144-3
Queen – Andrew Wild 978-1-78952-003-3
Radiohead – William Allen 978-1-78952-149-8
Rancid – Paul Matts 989-1-78952-187-0
Renaissance – David Detmer 978-1-78952-062-0
REO Speedwagon – Jim Romag 978-1-78952-262-4
The Rolling Stones 1963-80 – Steve Pilkington 978-1-78952-017-0
The Smiths and Morrissey – Tommy Gunnarsson 978-1-78952-140-5
Spirit – Rev. Keith A. Gordon – 978-1-78952- 248-8
Stackridge – Alan Draper 978-1-78952-232-7

Status Quo the Frantic Four Years – Richard James 978-1-78952-160-3
Steely Dan – Jez Rowden 978-1-78952-043-9
Steve Hackett – Geoffrey Feakes 978-1-78952-098-9
Tears For Fears – Paul Clark - 978-178952-238-9
Thin Lizzy – Graeme Stroud 978-1-78952-064-4
Tool – Matt Karpe 978-1-78952-234-1
Toto – Jacob Holm-Lupo 978-1-78952-019-4
U2 – Eoghan Lyng 978-1-78952-078-1
UFO – Richard James 978-1-78952-073-6
Van Der Graaf Generator – Dan Coffey 978-1-78952-031-6
Van Halen – Morgan Brown – 9781-78952-256-3
The Who – Geoffrey Feakes 978-1-78952-076-7
Roy Wood and the Move – James R Turner 978-1-78952-008-8
Yes – Stephen Lambe 978-1-78952-001-9
Frank Zappa 1966 to 1979 – Eric Benac 978-1-78952-033-0
Warren Zevon – Peter Gallagher 978-1-78952-170-2
10CC – Peter Kearns 978-1-78952-054-5

Decades Series

The Bee Gees in the 1960s – Andrew Mon Hughes et al 978-1-78952-148-1
The Bee Gees in the 1970s – Andrew Mon Hughes et al 978-1-78952-179-5
Black Sabbath in the 1970s – Chris Sutton 978-1-78952-171-9
Britpop – Peter Richard Adams and Matt Pooler 978-1-78952-169-6
Phil Collins in the 1980s – Andrew Wild 978-1-78952-185-6
Alice Cooper in the 1970s – Chris Sutton 978-1-78952-104-7
Alice Cooper in the 1980s – Chris Sutton 978-1-78952-259-4
Curved Air in the 1970s – Laura Shenton 978-1-78952-069-9
Donovan in the 1960s – Jeff Fitzgerald 978-1-78952-233-4
Bob Dylan in the 1980s – Don Klees 978-1-78952-157-3
Brian Eno in the 1970s – Gary Parsons 978-1-78952-239-6
Faith No More in the 1990s – Matt Karpe 978-1-78952-250-1
Fleetwood Mac in the 1970s – Andrew Wild 978-1-78952-105-4
Fleetwood Mac in the 1980s – Don Klees 978-178952-254-9
Focus in the 1970s – Stephen Lambe 978-1-78952-079-8
Free and Bad Company in the 1970s – John Van der Kiste 978-1-78952-178-8
Genesis in the 1970s – Bill Thomas 978178952-146-7
George Harrison in the 1970s – Eoghan Lyng 978-1-78952-174-0
Kiss in the 1970s – Peter Gallagher 978-1-78952-246-4
Manfred Mann's Earth Band in the 1970s – John Van der Kiste 978178952-243-3
Marillion in the 1980s – Nathaniel Webb 978-1-78952-065-1
Van Morrison in the 1970s – Peter Childs - 978-1-78952-241-9
Mott the Hoople and Ian Hunter in the 1970s –
John Van der Kiste 978-1-78-952-162-7

Pink Floyd In The 1970s – Georg Purvis 978-1-78952-072-9
Suzi Quatro in the 1970s – Darren Johnson 978-1-78952-236-5
Queen in the 1970s – James Griffiths 978-1-78952-265-5
Roxy Music in the 1970s – Dave Thompson 978-1-78952-180-1
Slade in the 1970s – Darren Johnson 978-1-78952-268-6
Status Quo in the 1980s – Greg Harper 978-1-78952-244-0
Tangerine Dream in the 1970s – Stephen Palmer 978-1-78952-161-0
The Sweet in the 1970s – Darren Johnson 978-1-78952-139-9
Uriah Heep in the 1970s – Steve Pilkington 978-1-78952-103-0
Van der Graaf Generator in the 1970s – Steve Pilkington 978-1-78952-245-7
Rick Wakeman in the 1970s – Geoffrey Feakes 978-1-78952-264-8
Yes in the 1980s – Stephen Lambe with David Watkinson 978-1-78952-125-2

On Screen series

Carry On... – Stephen Lambe 978-1-78952-004-0
David Cronenberg – Patrick Chapman 978-1-78952-071-2
Doctor Who: The David Tennant Years – Jamie Hailstone 978-1-78952-066-8
James Bond – Andrew Wild 978-1-78952-010-1
Monty Python – Steve Pilkington 978-1-78952-047-7
Seinfeld Seasons 1 to 5 – Stephen Lambe 978-1-78952-012-5

Other Books

1967: A Year In Psychedelic Rock 978-1-78952-155-9
1970: A Year In Rock – John Van der Kiste 978-1-78952-147-4
1973: The Golden Year of Progressive Rock 978-1-78952-165-8
Babysitting A Band On The Rocks – G.D. Praetorius 978-1-78952-106-1
Eric Clapton Sessions – Andrew Wild 978-1-78952-177-1
Derek Taylor: For Your Radioactive Children – Andrew Darlington 978-1-78952-038-5
The Golden Road: The Recording History of The Grateful Dead – John Kilbride 978-1-78952-156-6
Iggy and The Stooges On Stage 1967-1974 – Per Nilsen 978-1-78952-101-6
Jon Anderson and the Warriors – the road to Yes – David Watkinson 978-1-78952-059-0
Magic: The David Paton Story – David Paton 978-1-78952-266-2
Misty: The Music of Johnny Mathis – Jakob Baekgaard 978-1-78952-247-1
Nu Metal: A Definitive Guide – Matt Karpe 978-1-78952-063-7
Tommy Bolin: In and Out of Deep Purple – Laura Shenton 978-1-78952-070-5
Maximum Darkness – Deke Leonard 978-1-78952-048-4
The Twang Dynasty – Deke Leonard 978-1-78952-049-1

and many more to come!

Would you like to write for Sonicbond Publishing?

At Sonicbond Publishing we are always on the look-out for authors, particularly for our two main series:

On Track. Mixing fact with in depth analysis, the On Track series examines the work of a particular musical artist or group. All genres are considered from easy listening and jazz to 60s soul to 90s pop, via rock and metal.

On Screen. This series looks at the world of film and television. Subjects considered include directors, actors and writers, as well as entire television and film series. As with the On Track series, we balance fact with analysis.

While professional writing experience would, of course, be an advantage the most important qualification is to have real enthusiasm and knowledge of your subject. First-time authors are welcomed, but the ability to write well in English is essential.

Sonicbond Publishing has distribution throughout Europe and North America, and all books are also published in E-book form. Authors will be paid a royalty based on sales of their book.

Further details are available from www.sonicbondpublishing.co.uk. To contact us, complete the contact form there or email info@sonicbondpublishing.co.uk